Perfect
Speeches for
All Occasions

Matt Shinn

BOOKS

Published by Random House Books 2010
10 8 6 4 2 1 3 5 7 9

First published in the United Kingdom in 2010 by

ISBN 9781847945556

The Random House Group Limited supports The Forest Stewardship
Council® (FSC®), the leading international forest-certification organisation.
Our books carrying the FSC label are printed on FSC®-certified paper.
FSC is the only forest-certification scheme supported by the leading
environmental organisations, including Greenpeace. Our
paper procurement policy can be found at
www.randomhouse.co.uk/environment

MIX
Paper from
responsible sources
FSC® C018072

Typeset by Palimpsest Book Production Limited, Grangemouth, Stirlingshire

Printed and bound in Great Britain by Clays Ltd, St Ives plc

Contents

Acknowledgements

The author would like to thank Lucy Brett and Robin Parker for letting him reproduce their wedding speech.

Introduction

'Oh ****, I've got to give a speech!'

For many people, speaking in public is their idea of hell. It features among the ten most common phobias: 'public speaking' even comes out higher than 'death' in surveys of the things that people are most scared of. So at a funeral, many people would rather be the one in the coffin than the one who has to give the eulogy.

And like death, giving speeches is hard to avoid. It's difficult to get very far, either professionally or socially, without being able to speak well in public. To be successful in most walks of life, it's just something that you have to do.

But let's not dwell on the 'have to'. There are enormous benefits to be gained from being a good speaker. A couple of recent examples show just what a difference it can make.

Winning words - the noteless wonder

Take David Cameron's speech at the Conservative Party Conference in 2005, a speech which was instrumental in his winning the leadership of his party.

The Tories were about to begin the contest to decide who would be their next leader, and therefore potentially the next prime minister. Each of the main contenders had the chance to make a speech at the conference, which marked the real start of the leadership contest.

Leading up to the conference, the bookies' favourite had been David Davis, who was believed to have the support of the majority of Conservative MPs. But all the party members had a say in the final decision, and so having the opportunity to speak to them directly was extremely important. Everything hinged on the ability of the candidates to sell themselves as potential leaders.

David Davis was first up, but his speech was lacking in spark. He came across as wooden, as he stood stiffly behind his lectern, reading from a prepared text. Sometimes he tripped over his words. Often he looked down after making an important point, rather than looking his audience in the eye. His face wasn't animated or open – most of the time it was set in a kind of scowl. All in all, he didn't look as if he was having a good time.

And when it came to the content of his speech, commentators remarked upon the 'dead weight of the bleeding obvious' that dragged his words down like a pair of concrete wellingtons.

David Cameron, by contrast, came out with a message about the need for modernisation and reform, about the need to 'look, feel, think and behave like a completely new organisation', and he backed this message up with a bold speaking style.

He didn't use notes (though he'd clearly prepared his speech with enormous care, and had memorised it). Instead of standing behind a lectern he roamed around the stage, he came up close to his audience, and he reinforced his points with open gestures. Everything about him – his body language, his facial expression, his words – spoke of an earnest desire to communicate; of a confidence in himself, a belief in what he was saying, and an urgency in getting it across.

Within 24 hours of the two speeches, the bookies had changed their minds and made Cameron the odds-on favourite, having been ten to one against. He went on to win convincingly.

Getting the Games - with a speech

Or look at Lord Coe's magnificent speech to International Olympic Committee delegates in Singapore in 2005, which helped win the 2012 Games for London.

Again, London wasn't the bookies' favourite prior to the speech, and there was nothing really new to say about the bid itself – the plans for the London Games had been presented in enormous detail over many months.

So what did Lord Coe talk about? He told a very personal story.

'When I was twelve years old, I was marched into a large school hall with my classmates, and we watched grainy pictures from the 1968 Mexico Olympic Games,' he said. 'Two athletes from our home town were competing. John Sherwood won a bronze medal in the 400m hurdles. His wife Sheila just narrowly missed gold in the long jump. By the time I was back in my classroom, I knew what I wanted to do, and what I wanted to be. Thirty-five years on, I stand before you with those memories still fresh. Still inspired by this great movement.'

The London Games, he said, would be about inspiring young people in just the same way as he'd been inspired, all those years ago.

The cleverness of this speech lay in Lord Coe's understanding of who his audience was. Practically every member of the IOC is a former athlete: every one of them, in other words, has their own personal equivalent of the moment of inspiration that Lord Coe was talking about.

For all the detail concerning investment and logistics which was set out in the bids, and for all the high technology that the 2012 Games will involve, it was an appeal to the emotions, delivered by someone standing up and speaking about his own life, which swung it for London. Lord Coe may not have used the flowery rhetoric of some of the great speeches of the past, but his speech is still a great example of what you can achieve with mere words.

The power of the spoken word

Of course, both David Cameron and Lord Coe are seasoned public speakers who are used to talking in front of large audiences. But writing and giving a powerful speech is something that most people can do. Really.

In the old days, schoolchildren were routinely taught the art of rhetoric, as something that they would need in order to make successes of themselves. Few of us now get this kind of preparation, but by putting in some work and developing this skill, you too can achieve what you want by speaking well.

- You might want to do a good job of officiating or being guest of honour at an event.

- You might want to use your speech to campaign for a political cause (politics is about engaging with large groups of people, after all, and you can't get far as a politician without being able to move an audience, at least with the help of a decent speechwriter).

- You might want to help a voluntary or charitable organisation, a pressure group or representative body, to gain media attention and win public support.

- You might want to get publicity for your business – speeches can be far more effective in shaping people's perceptions than slick advertising.

- You might want to stake your own claim to be a leader or potential leader.

- You might want to impress your potential employer with your speaking skills, as part of a job selection process.

- Or you might just want to make people happy at a wedding.

Using the right words in the right order can change things, and the good news is that the elements that make up a great speech are pretty much what they've always been. The art of rhetoric is ancient – well over 2,000 years old.

Our powers of communication now might seem to eclipse anything we've had before. We can send messages instantly around the world by fax, mobile phone and email, but the people who are receiving these messages are still human. You can talk to someone on the other side of the world, but that doesn't mean that they'll listen to you.

Impact is what speeches are good for, and what they've always been good for. Speeches are about motivating people and moving them, about making your message hit home. For all the technology that we have at our disposal, there's still a primal power in the ability of someone to stand up in front of an audience, to speak, and to speak well.

Partly it's a question of trust. These days it's so easy to use technology to give a false impression of the truth. But a good speaker stands in front of an audience armed only with a few pieces of paper, and relies entirely on the strength of the argument that they're going to put forward. Giving a speech means that your audience can see the whites of your eyes.

A great speech can be poetry and drama all in one. It can make the hairs on a listener's neck stand up. It can inspire people, give them ideas, give them courage. Hearing a fine speaker really carrying an audience with them, just by the force of their words and their own skill in delivering them, can be a mesmerising experience. That is the extraordinary and enduring power of the spoken word. And that's why, as we'll see, sometimes the most effective thing is not to spruce your speech up with the latest technological gadgetry.

Above all, a good speech makes people think better of the person who's given it. The ability to speak well in public does wonders for your standing, whether at work or in your personal life.

I hope that this book will help you to build your confidence in public speaking, and to understand what will engage your audience, and what will influence, entertain and impress them. Speaking in public isn't rocket science, and most people underestimate their own ability to do it. Luckily, most of the things that go to make up a good speech are things that you have control over. They take a little bit of work. But when things go spectacularly wrong, they are nearly always the speaker's own fault. They're to do with being overconfident, with coming across as arrogant and patronising, with not doing enough homework on your subject and who you're talking to. All avoidable.

This book can help you to find the words to carry your audience with you, to persuade them and inspire them. It points you towards rhetorical tricks and tools that have proved their effectiveness over many centuries, and have been used by some of the greatest speakers in history. You might not be the next Barack Obama, but with preparation you can still be an excellent public speaker.

How to use this book

In this book we'll go through the stages that most speechwriting follows: finding out about the event you're speaking at and about your audience; deciding on the main things that you want your speech to accomplish; working out a logical structure for your material; adding jokes and other embellishments; varying your pace and tone to keep it interesting; adding a few sound bites to sum up what you've been saying; and building up to a big finish. But there aren't any hard-and-fast rules when it comes to giving a speech. Every audience is different, and every one is made up of a different mix of people.

No speech book can tell you what to write (and the ones that claim they can are best avoided). The tips in this book aren't arbitrary – they're based on techniques that have been shown to work over many centuries. But they are only tools, to help you speak now, in the 21st century, in your own voice; to help you find your own best way of communicating with your audience.

And in the end, the audience is always right. Their reaction is the only test of whether a speech is any good or not. Have they taken on board what you want them to? Have they laughed in the right places? Have they followed you to the end? Have they taken the right things home with them?

But not necessarily, 'Do they think you're a good speaker?' It can be a bit of a double-edged compliment if someone says to you afterwards, 'You're great at giving speeches, aren't you?' What you want is 'I thought what you said about the groom was really touching.' Or 'I was really interested in what you said about x.' Or 'I absolutely agree with you about y.' Speaking well is only the means to this end.

These days especially, one of the most dangerous things you can do as a speaker is to make speaking seem to come too easily to you: to look as if you can fake the passion when you need to. There are no prizes for sounding glib. It's been the Achilles heel of a few politicians over the years – fantastic orators, who have just a touch of the snake oil salesman about them.

It doesn't really matter if you come across as a bit nervous or hesitant – what's more important is that you don't put on an act. You have to give your audience something of yourself – what you really think and feel, the way that you (at your best) would really put it. If this book has a single message, it's that you should trust yourself, and be confident in speaking without putting on airs and graces.

When you give a speech, you can't go far wrong if you come across as the person that you really are. Say the things that sound natural for you, avoid sounding as if you're trying to be someone else, and you'll be all right.

> *My father gave me these hints on speech-making: 'Be sincere . . . be brief . . . be seated.'* James Roosevelt

In the end it's all about sincerity. And as the saying goes, 'if you can fake that, you've got it made'.

1 Preparation, preparation, preparation

The secret of a good speech lies in the work you put in before you give it. As Abraham Lincoln said, 'Give me six hours to chop down a tree and I will spend the first four sharpening the axe.'

First things first – the event, and your part in it

So D-Day is marked in your diary: the date on which your rhetorical skills will be unleashed upon an unsuspecting world. One of the first things you'll need to do is to understand the nature of the event that you've been asked to speak at, and therefore what will be appropriate in terms of tone and content. You'll need also to find out about practicalities. The following is a checklist of things you may need to consider.

Checklist: the event

- What time are you on, and how long are you on for?

- Where is the venue, and how long will it take you to reach it? (You don't want to be flustered by having to race to get there, or – God forbid – arrive late.)

- Who will introduce you? Will you be able to talk to this person in advance, to make sure that what they'll say about you is accurate?

- Who's on before you, and who's on after?

> - Will there be time for questions, and if so, will they come immediately after your speech, or will you take them together with some of the other speakers?
> - What visual aids, if any, will you be able to use?
> - Will you need to use a microphone to reach the back of the room, or to be heard over ambient noise in the venue?

Using your time to prepare

Of course, one of the first things you'll want to work out is how long you've got to prepare for your speech.

Say you've got a speech coming up in two weeks' time. The temptation might be to get it all written as soon as you can. But the best speeches are often those which have been mulled over for the longest time.

> *It usually takes more than three weeks to prepare a good impromptu speech.* Mark Twain

Don't rush. Don't try to have it all done a week before you have to give it. Give yourself time, especially to work out the overall shape of your speech, and to decide what you ultimately want it to do. Sleep on it. Think about it in the bath.

It's amazing how, when you know the outline of what you want to talk about, your brain can be working away on it without you realising. You'll start noticing things that you read or hear which are relevant to the subject you'll be talking about, and which could make your speech sound topical. If you can, allow time for this to happen.

Seeing is believing - visual aids

At an early stage, you'll need to find out from the event organisers what equipment is likely to be available, and hence whether you can use visuals to support your talk. You need to know not just whether they have equipment, but what type it is, and whether it's capable of doing what you might need it to do.

We'll come to what makes an effective visual accompaniment to a speech later. At this stage all you need to decide is whether, if the venue can accommodate it, you want to speak alongside slides or props or not.

Interspersing your speech with visuals can, if done well, make it more interesting and informative. It's the same principle that TV news programmes use to try to keep their audience's attention: mixing up words and pictures.

Using visuals can also be a very good way of making your point. Your speech may use a lot of statistics, or it may explain complex processes that would be easier to represent visually. Sometimes, visuals also have greater truth-value than the spoken word – your listeners may be more likely to believe something that they can see, rather than something they've only heard about.

You'll need to bear in mind, though, that using visuals adds an element of fiddling about that you could possibly do without, especially when you're nervous. They're another thing that can go wrong. They can be very distracting to an audience, who may switch off from what they're hearing. And continually having to look down to bring up the next PowerPoint slide on your computer, or turning to check that your projector is showing things the right way up, breaks your eye contact with the people you're speaking to, and makes it more difficult to engage with them.

It's unlikely that your speech really *needs* visuals. Most of the great orators throughout history did just fine without them. Will images support your speech and increase its impact, or will they compete with it? If you're in doubt, leave them out. And if you do plan to use visuals, you'll need to remember the golden rule as you write your speech and prepare the visuals themselves: always assume the worst. Assume that after all your hard work in getting your slides together, you'll arrive at the venue and something will be wrong with the equipment, so that you can't show anything. You need to make sure that your speech makes sense in its own right, and that if you're reduced to the lowest of low technology – your words scribbled down on paper – the speech will still work.

If you do opt for visuals, there are all kinds of equipment that you can use, from the truly primitive (props, blackboards and flip charts) through to whizzy multimedia programs that allow you to play video clips as well as show slides. Which you choose will depend partly on what your venue can accommodate, what suits the content of your speech, and your personal style as a speaker.

At the bottom of the technological tree, there are props. Using objects in speeches has a long history, and can be very effective.

When William Wilberforce was campaigning against the slave trade, he was arguing against people who claimed that many slaves were happy with their conditions, and were well looked after. Wilberforce used to carry with him a set of bloodied manacles that had been used to keep slaves from running away. He had them on show next to him as he spoke, a constant visual reminder that things weren't quite so rosy on the plantations as his opponents made out.

Props, being actual objects, can have an impact that illustrations can't. They have high curiosity value for audiences. But they can be bulky, they tend to be static and unchanging, and they can be hard to see from a distance.

At the next level, blackboards and flip charts are good when your main purpose is to impart a lot of information to your listeners, or where you want to capture suggestions from them (in a brainstorming session, for example). The advantage of blackboards and flip charts is that they stop you getting ahead of yourself. Writing things out takes time, and it generally keeps pace with what you're talking about. And it's not like bringing up a new PowerPoint slide, where everyone's attention is instantly diverted to what they can see, and away from what you're saying.

But you're not going to wow anyone with a blackboard. You won't be able to reach the back of a large hall with a flip chart. It's difficult to write anything on either of them without turning your back on your audience. And while having things pre-written on a flip chart has a certain homespun charm, it's too informal for most speeches: it just looks as if you haven't bothered to prepare better visuals that could be projected on a screen.

In a nutshell, blackboards and flip charts are good for teachers, trainers and people running brainstorming meetings, but bad for platform speakers.

Slides and transparencies on overhead projectors are marginally better, but using them is fiddly, and increasingly retro. These days, if you're going to use visuals, PowerPoint presentations (or those using similar software packages – there are several) are what you should think about. But beware – just because you can make slides in different colours, with all kinds of amusing little cartoons and with lines of text swooping in one after another, it doesn't mean that you should do so. It's easy for the content of a speech to be swamped when there's too much going on visually. 'Death by PowerPoint', we speechwriters call it.

Length – how long is too long?

Another thing you'll want to find out early on is how long you're expected to speak for. This will affect how much you can plan to cover in your speech. If you have a time limit, you need to make sure that you don't go on longer than you should. If you don't have a limit, it is still important not to try your audience's patience. Brevity is the soul of wit, as the fellow said, and it's the soul of a good speech.

This is where you might need to be disciplined. The best speech isn't always the one that crams the most in. The Gettysburg Address, one of the most famous and widely quoted speeches in history, is only 270 words long. And as we'll see, there are limits to what the average audience can take in. Have you ever heard someone say that a speech was too short?

Avoid the temptation to tell your audience everything you know about your subject. Giving people too much to take in can mean that they take away less from your speech, not more.

To help you fill your slot but not run over, bear in mind that most people speak at somewhere between 120 and 150 words a minute. This is an average, of course – in practice there will be passages where you speak faster (most people speed up when they're recounting anecdotes, for example) and parts where you will want to slow down and even pause for emphasis (especially to help drive home a key point).

As a rule of thumb, though, if you're scheduled to speak for ten minutes you should be making your way to the podium with no more than about 1,500 words to deliver.

What speeches are good for, and what they're not good for

Speeches are better for some things than others. Broadly speaking, they're good for drama, for vision, for emotion. They're good for the big picture.

Speeches are about presenting the key facts, the best examples, the most persuasive arguments. They're about the instant hit. Half an hour after your presentation, most of your listeners won't remember much of what you said. But if you get it right, they'll long remember how you made them feel.

What speeches are not good for is conveying loads of detail. Listening to someone speaking from a dense piece of text, which has been written to be read and not heard, will send most audiences off to the land of Nod. Complex information is better got from books. But what you can do in a speech is make your listeners want to go and read those books.

> *Eloquence is the essential thing in a speech, not information.*
> Mark Twain

So don't overload your speech. Talk in the best way you can about what matters most; set this out as clearly and concisely as you can, then vamoose.

Writing it down first - why it's a good idea

Good public speaking is more than just talking: the best speeches generally aren't improvised (even when they sound as if they are). The process of thinking about your speech beforehand, and writing it out, allows you to develop your ideas much further than if you were just to stand up and wing it.

Writing your speech out before you deliver it gives you confidence – you know that what you are about to say really does represent your considered view on your subject, expressed in the best way that you can express it, after long deliberation.

Writing your words down first also allows you to structure them in the most effective way to fit the time you have, with changes in mood and tone, with your arguments in a logical order, and with a pleasing, organic shape, including a proper beginning, middle and end.

So, even if you're not going to be using speaking notes, write your speech out first.

Speaking notes or full text?

One of the other things you need to decide at an early stage is the kind of speaking notes, if any, that you'll want to take in with you when you give your speech.

A speech that is written out in full, with every sentence weighed and pondered over, can be a great security blanket. You know that even if your mind goes blank, nothing's going to wipe the ink from those precious pages. You know that you have the fruits of your careful thought right there in your hand, and even if you fluff the delivery you know that the words you're saying sum up your ideas as well as possible. Some modern lecterns have glass screens that reflect your words at eye-level without your audience being able to see them, allowing you to read from a full text without having to look down.

Speaking from a full text also helps you to avoid putting your foot in it with phrases that could be taken the wrong way, or that may cause unintentional offence. As you read your speech through at the rehearsal stage, you can watch out for anything unfortunate.

A full text enables you to structure your speech more carefully – you can decide on the exact balance between the different sections, and tweak the pacing as you rehearse it, to build to a climax at the end. This is trickier to do from short notes, especially for an inexperienced speaker.

Speaking from a full text helps you to make your points more concisely – by going over your draft a few times you can boil your arguments down to their essence, and cut out all the unnecessary little words and pauses that litter most people's speech when they're speaking on their feet.

A full text also helps you to fill your speaking slot more precisely – you can work out exactly how long it takes you to deliver your speech this way. If timekeeping is likely to be strict at the event you're speaking at, this could help you avoid having to lose an important point rather than overrunning.

Finally, reading from a full text can be useful if you're planning to publicise your speech. You know exactly what you said and what you didn't, and hey presto, you've got a ready-made record of your words to hand to the waiting press or to your publishers.

However, sometimes it can be more effective to speak from shorter speaking notes, or even to talk without any visible means of support, without notes at all. You may have memorised every single word of what you want to say, but by using minimal notes you send out a lot of positive signals.

Your speech will be more interesting for sounding (at least in part) spontaneous. Speaking only from short notes, or without notes at all, makes you look as if you genuinely want to engage with your audience – you're looking them in the eye, you're approaching this as a conversation, and you're ready to respond to them, and to any issues that crop up. You look competent – you have so much command over your material that you don't need to have it written down. You look sincere – you're coming before the audience 'unarmed', relying only on your deeply held convictions. And you look confident – you're so convinced of the value of what you're going to say that you're prepared to back yourself to deliver it successfully.

In practice, of course, you can combine elements of both methods – having parts where you're prepared to speak extempore, but also having detailed notes in front of you (especially of quotations, statistics, and your opening and closing sections) to bring you back to your theme if you're in danger of going off on a tangent, and to make sure that you cover everything. Like a good comedian's act, the best speeches will often move from scripted material to ad lib and back again, without anyone seeing the join.

The approach you should choose depends to a large extent on the nature of your speech and what you want to achieve by giving it. David Cameron's speaking-without-notes approach worked well because the speech was largely about *him*. It depends also on your confidence and how good you are at thinking on your feet when the pressure's on. If you have any suspicion that you might dry up, write out your speech in full and take it with you.

Know thy audience – who are they, and how are you going to reach them?

Speeches don't take place in a vacuum. The key to public speaking is to understand your audience, and to do everything in your power to engage with them. To manage this, you need first to know who they are.

Checklist: the audience

- Have the audience been specially invited, or is the event open to the general public?

- What motivates the people who are there – what interests them?

- How much do they already know about your subject?

- How are you going to frame your arguments so that they address the things that matter to these people?

- Which things can you take for granted that your audience *don't* need to be convinced of?

- Who is an authority to these people?

- What everyday realities do they understand, and which of these could you relate your arguments to?

- Which cultural or local references will mean something to them?

Knowing your listeners can involve knowing how old they are; people at different stages of life have different levels of life experience, and they're preoccupied by different things. The frames of reference that they have, and even the kinds of conversational language that they're used to, may be different.

The size of an audience is another important factor when you are preparing a speech. A large audience generally suggests a more formal occasion, meaning in turn that you should be a little more formal in your language and delivery, reining in some of your more idiomatic phrases, and maybe using a few more of the classic rhetorical techniques that we'll come to later.

Think about your audience members too in terms of the professional or political affiliation that they may have, and whether they are drawn in large part from any particular faith groups or interest groups. This information can help you to avoid alienating your audience, and to connect with them better – if you know that many of your listeners don't speak English as a first language, for example, you can be careful to avoid using colloquial phrases in your speech.

Rarely should there be any major surprises when it comes to the make-up of your audience. Since you've been asked to speak, you should be able to find out exactly what the event is, who has been invited to listen, and why those people will have come – what they want to get out of it.

Audiences are always mixed, but you're looking for common threads that connect your different listeners. By working out their shared pre-occupations and concerns, you're identifying the buttons that you can press with them.

On the most basic level, you're also trying to work out whether your audience will start out as generally friendly towards you and receptive to what you're saying, neutral, or (as sometimes happens) actively hostile. Knowing this will help you to determine how much time and effort you need to put into winning your audience over, especially in the early part of your speech, and gaining their trust. With a hostile or suspicious audience this will be half the battle. With more friendly ones you can head much more quickly to the subjects that you want to talk about.

None of this means, though, that you should act as if you are part of the same group as your audience, if you're clearly not. There are few things more cringe-making than hearing speakers trying to ingratiate themselves with their listeners, by copying their particular ways of speaking. Your job is to communicate clearly with your audience, not necessarily to pass yourself off as one of them. So you shouldn't try to imitate the speech patterns of an age group that you don't belong to, for example, but you should at least be aware of anything in your natural way of speaking that your audience might have trouble following.

Building your speech - the bottom line

Having analysed the event and your audience, you now need to decide what you want your speech to do. What's your ultimate aim?

Checklist: the aim

- To persuade your audience of something?

- To publicise your business?

- To get people to vote, think or act a certain way?

- To draw attention to a particular cause or organisation?

- To inspire your flagging workforce?

- To raise your own profile, and be acknowledged as an authority on a subject?

- To embarrass the groom, but in a way that's funny and actually quite sweet?

What change are you trying to bring about in your audience? If they're entirely the same after listening to you, you've wasted their time as well as your own.

Of course, a speech can do more than one thing at the same time, but it's asking a lot if you have more than two or three main objectives. Even then, you probably won't achieve all of them, but you give yourself the best chance if you have a clear idea about priorities. Whatever your overall aims, it's a good idea to have them written down somewhere for you to consult at a later stage, to make sure that you're keeping to plan.

Choosing a theme and thinking up a title

Of all the things that you could possibly talk about, you need to choose the right one for this occasion. To do this, there are two basic things to consider.

First, you need to find a subject that you care about, and even feel passionate about. It's very difficult to engage an audience unless you're speaking on a subject that engages *you*. Even if you've spoken on this general subject many times before, you need to find some new angle that enlivens it for you, so that you can do your audience the courtesy of sounding interested in your speech yourself.

Then, within this broad subject area, you need to identify points of common ground between what you want to talk about, and what your audience might be interested in hearing about. There has to be something in it for you, and something in it for them.

One way of giving a focus to your ideas about your theme is to decide at an early stage what the title of your speech is going to be. In many cases, this will be the first communication that you have with your audience – they'll see your title printed in their event programme, for example. It will play an important role in letting them know what to expect, and even in persuading them to turn up for your presentation rather than sloping off for a crafty cigarette and saving their attention for someone else on the bill. Your speech title therefore needs to be engaging and interesting, while still representing accurately what your speech is about, so that people who do come to hear you don't feel short-changed.

Try to make your speech title intriguing. You don't need to give away everything that you're going to speak about – you can tease your audience a little, and leave something to their imagination.

It helps if your title at least starts with something brief and eye-catching. Titles that can be read at a glance are much more effective than long ones. If you feel that you need to do a little more to explain what your speech is about, you can always do it through a subtitle, following your attention-grabbing opener.

Titles can take many forms. You can use well-known quotations ('And so I face the final curtain: twenty years in show business'). You can start with a challenging or beguiling question. Jokes and puns in titles are good, as they hold out the promise that coming and listening to you may be an enjoyable experience. First person narrative is good too – 'I was a . . .'.

If you're stuck for ideas, look at the way that journalists in some of the better quality papers use teasing and punning titles to get people to read their articles. They face many of the same problems that you do in thinking up a title for a speech – summing up a complex argument in a way that encourages the reader to find out more – and many of the tricks they use will work for you too.

Even if your speech doesn't need a title, it can still be helpful to think of what title you *would* have given it. A good title provides something for your ideas to cohere around, and having one is a useful first step in the process of structuring your speech, helping to keep you from straying too far from your subject.

Playing with your title is also a good way of getting your head round the speech that will follow it. Even small tweaks to the wording of a title can make you see your subject in quite a different way. Getting the title right should help you to clarify exactly what you want your speech to cover.

Prioritise – why it never pays to overestimate your audience

Experiments show that even the brightest audiences find it extremely difficult to remember much of what they've actually heard in a speech. Most people will come away with a vague memory of your overall themes, and maybe one or two of your more memorable lines. But that's about it: no audience has total recall.

These limitations on your listeners' memories mean that it's a good idea to decide, early in the writing process, what are the two or three points that you want to make absolutely sure that people take away with them when they hear you. You can then use the structure and style of your speech to give yourself the best chance of making these ideas stick.

Gathering material

Now that you've chosen your theme and have a title around which to crystallise your thoughts, you're ready to begin gathering information for your speech, drawing together the anecdotes, examples and illustrations that will help to bring it to life. Carrying out research can be time-consuming, but it's one of the most important stages of writing your speech, and you dispense with it at your peril.

The first research resource to turn to is the one that's closest to hand: your own head. It can be surprising how much you find that you know about a subject once you start mining your own experience, and this is often the kind of first-hand material that works well in speeches. Dredging it all up can take some doing, though. Make sure that you keep a notebook by you, for all those awkward moments when stories and ideas pop into your mind, and do whatever it is that makes your ideas flow easily. Going for walks by yourself is a time-honoured method; driving, typing and long soaks in the bath work for some people too.

As you make your internal survey of everything you know about your subject, you might start to notice gaps that need filling. Even if you don't, extra research for your speech can help you make it especially relevant for the occasion. It can also give you up-to-date material that shows you've done some preparation, and help to refresh the topic for you if you already know it inside out.

These days, of course, using the internet is the quickest way to find quotations on specific subjects and a wide range of other material useful for your speech. The web needs to be treated with some caution, however. Always try to check the original source before using statistics that you've found. Similarly, if you come across a quotation that would be useful to you, try to find out about the credentials of the person you're quoting, and what organisation they're part of. There are a lot of strange people out there.

With any information that you find on the web, check whether it is consistent with other sources, whether it is up-to-date, and whether it appears to be objective. If it represents an individual's point of view, but not necessarily that of the organisation that they're part of, you need to say so.

And don't neglect other secondary sources. Libraries can be an excellent resource, especially those with searchable databases of articles in the press, which give you speedy access to extended treatments of your subject.

Other basic materials that will help you with your speech include a good standard dictionary (you should never rely on your computer's spellchecker, and searching online for even the most eccentric spelling of a word will usually throw up at least a few examples). A thesaurus can make your speech sound more elegant, as you can avoid continually using the same words, but make sure you're aware of the different connotations of the words that are listed as alternatives, and confident in the pronunciation and meaning of any you decide to use.

The specialist press can be a useful resource when you're speaking to particular interest groups, while local newspapers can provide you with topical references when you're talking in a specific locality, and give you an idea of the issues that are of immediate interest to your listeners.

And don't neglect the value of just talking to people, whether in person or on the phone. It looks good if you've gone off and interviewed someone especially for your speech; if you've done that, make sure your audience know that you've done it.

2 Getting the structure right

So you've analysed your audience, worked out exactly what you want to achieve by speaking, found a catchy title for your speech, and researched your subject. Now comes the easy part – writing the thing.

Only it isn't quite as simple as that. Before you get started, there's something that you need: a plan. You need to put together the framework of your speech, on which you'll hang what you're going to say. Ultimately this will speed up the writing process, and your speech will end up much more effective for a bit of organisation at the outset.

Your audience can't rewind – making your speech memorable

The thing to remember is that speeches are different from other forms of communication. If you're talking to a live audience and their attention starts to wander, they can't just go back to the beginning like they can with a magazine article, to remind themselves of what you've been talking about. You have only one chance to get your audience to pay attention, and to understand and remember what you have to say.

More than anything else, it is structure that will help your audience follow what you're saying. And by structuring your speech properly, you make it much more likely that your words will stick in the minds of your listeners.

Remembering things is always easier when they are connected in a logical narrative: that's why it's important that your speech fits together in a way that makes sense. You should try to include stories in your speech to illustrate your point, but you should also aim to ensure that your whole speech tells a story, that it has a 'narrative arc'. A common narrative structure found in speeches is 'attention-problem-solution' – first you grab your audience's attention, then you give examples of a problem that needs to be confronted, and you finish with the solution you're proposing.

Similarly, making ideas concrete means they're more likely to sink in, so make sure that you give yourself space to paint pictures with your words, and explain the practical implications of what you're talking about, in real nuts-and-bolts terms. Franklin D. Roosevelt once said in a speech: 'I hate war . . . I have seen war on land and sea. I have seen blood running from the wounded. I have seen men coughing out their gassed lungs. I have seen the dead in the mud. I have seen cities destroyed . . . I have seen children starving. I have seen the agony of mothers and wives. I hate war.' If he had just said 'I hate war' he would have saved time, but he wouldn't have been nearly as convincing or memorable.

It helps if there aren't too many things to remember in your speech, and repetition makes it easier to remember them. So if there are points that you want to make sure your audience take away with them, you should use the structure of your speech to reiterate them. Consider Winston Churchill's advice to the future Edward VIII: 'If you have an important point to make, don't try to be subtle or clever. Use a pile driver. Hit the point once. Then come back and hit it again. Then hit it a third time – a tremendous whack.'

Associating an idea with strong emotion also makes it more likely to be remembered. You might want to wait for a particularly tear-jerking or tub-thumping bit of your speech before introducing it.

Finally, the more unexpected and unusual something is, the more it stands out, and the more memorable it's likely to be. As we'll see later, you can use the structure and rhythm of your speech to build up to important ideas or phrases – called 'sparklers' in the trade – and make them really prominent.

So structure helps to make your words clear, and it helps to make your speech memorable. Structure also helps to keep you on track when you feel tempted to waffle and digress. With some kinds of speech – wedding speeches for example – the structure is imposed on you, to a certain degree. The formalities mean that there are certain things you have to say, in a certain order, and certain specific things that your speech has to do. But in any speech, getting the structure right is one of the main ways of ensuring that you do a good job.

Having an outline forces you to plan and organise your thoughts, to determine in advance what you intend to say, and to begin at the beginning. The outline serves as a framework for your full, developed speech, giving it shape and structure. And it helps you to maintain a clear theme throughout your speech – speeches with a single, strong line of argument are the easiest to follow, and tend to be the most powerful. Whatever happens, don't rush in and start scribbling before you have your structure all worked out.

As we go through the different phases of a typical speech, you might want to jot down somewhere – the back of an envelope is traditional – your ideas for the basic outline of the speech you're planning to give. If you're having trouble getting your ideas together in a narrative, try writing them out on separate slips of paper and moving them around to change the order. Not only will this process help you to structure your speech as you write it, but it will also give you some rough speaking notes when you come to deliver it, if you don't want to read from a full text.

Your introduction

Giving a speech is like telling a story, and as every schoolchild knows, a story needs a beginning, a middle and an end. Similarly, every speech-writer knows that you have to 'tell them what you're going to tell them, tell them, and then tell them what you've told them'. This all makes perfect sense. But unfortunately, it leaves out a very important part of a speech – maybe *the* most important part – the introduction. And the introduction isn't the same as the beginning.

It's a bad idea to dive right in, and get straight to the meat of your speech, for a number of reasons. When you start speaking, most people in the audience will spend the first few moments getting used to the way you talk. Some latecomers may still be finding their seats, and they'll need a while to gather their wits and stop distracting everyone else. But more than this, as you begin speaking, your audience will be preoccupied with sizing you up. First impressions are important in speeches – the first few words that the audience hears from you will affect how they respond to the whole of the rest of your speech. What you say at the outset can make them warm to you, take an interest in you, trust you – or it can put them off for good.

That's why you need a good introduction, to soften your audience up before you hit them with what you really want to say. There are various ways of doing this, but what they have in common is that they're all aimed at establishing a connection between you and your audience: they're all ways of telling your audience that it's worth listening to you.

Whichever approach you choose for your introduction, aim for a big opening – wheel out your best gag, your most striking fact, your warmest and most touchy-feely list of thank yous. You can always combine them – a list of thanks followed by a good joke works wonders. But don't apologise for what you are going to say, and don't plead for sympathy if you're 'unaccustomed to public speaking'. And whatever you do, don't start your speech by reading out the title that you've chosen for it – it makes you sound like you're in primary school.

I'd like to thank ...

One of the best options for your introduction is to start by saying your thank yous. There's the person who introduced you, plus the people who organised the event you're speaking at. Praise your host, praise the venue you're speaking in, praise the locality you're speaking in.

If you want to be asked back, it's always a good idea to keep in with the event organisers who have paid you the compliment of asking you to speak. And it's nice to be nice. But there's another reason why it can be good to start with a list of thanks. A good thank you makes you look like an insider. It makes you look as if you're an integral part of the event that you're speaking at. It makes you look generous, clued-up and sociable. That's why it can be effective if you start by name-checking individuals. It makes them feel good, but it also makes you look good.

It's the same as when politicians at party rallies single out individuals in the crowd and point at them, as if to say 'Great, *you're* here!' Maybe they're not pointing at anyone in particular. Maybe the person they're pointing at has no idea who they are. But to the rest of the audience, it makes them look friendly and popular. And being the fickle creatures that they are, this makes the audience more disposed to like them, and to listen to what they have to say.

It looks good if you can weave in a reference to what the speaker before you has said (even if it means thinking on your feet) – it shows you've been listening. You can name-check places too – if you can show that you know the locality, by making topical references to what's been going on there, it can make an audience view you more favourably.

Of course, if you're going to name-check people and places, it's absolutely crucial that the names that you check are the right names.

Making them sit up and listen

Another classic way of starting a speech is to try to make your audience notice you. Start your speech with something that grabs their attention. This could be an anecdote, a quote or a question.

When you're speaking to a live audience, you're always battling against the forces of distraction. The people you're speaking to may be tired and listless. They might have just come back from lunch (early afternoon is the graveyard shift for speakers, and the one to be avoided if you can). There may be someone next to them who's a fidget or who has a particularly annoying cough.

To get your audience to sit up and listen, you can use what in the USA they call a 'grabber'. Something striking and interesting; something that will make people forget how uncomfortable their seats are, or how much they fancy the person sitting in front of them. It could be a physical thing – the CEO of a well-known motorcycle company sometimes rides up to the lectern on one of his own machines, which is certainly dramatic. It could be a rhetorical question, a controversial statement or a challenge. It could involve standing at the lectern in silence, clicking your fingers every few seconds, to represent the number of deaths caused by preventable diseases in developing countries.

If everyone else is using high-tech visuals, grabbing people's attention could involve something as simple as just standing and talking to your audience. Or if everyone else is using very dry statistics, telling a few stories with real people in them.

You might need to surprise your listeners, particularly if you've spoken to them before. Audiences always have expectations. If they've heard you already, they may think they know what to expect. Even if they haven't heard you, they may associate you with other speakers they've heard from the organisation you represent. You have to break through their preconceptions, to surprise them.

However you do it, the aim is to startle, to intrigue, to make a forceful claim on your audience's attention. It takes a degree of confidence, but if it's done well it can be very effective.

Starting with a good gag

We'll come to the role of humour in speeches – what makes a good joke, and what to do if your audience doesn't laugh at it – later. But for the purposes of an introduction, few things work as well as a well-aimed gag. If you can keep it fairly short, all the better. If you can work in references to the locality or the event, or to things that your audience are interested in, better still. Combine all this with a bit of self-mockery, and they'll be eating out of your hand.

The beginning – tell them what you're going to tell them ...

The beginning of your speech is your chance to give your audience a preview of what's coming up. They'll know what's in store, and where you're going with your theme.

Getting your beginning right helps you write your speech, because it gives you the central theme or idea around which everything else is organised. And it starts the process of reiteration, the repetition of your key points that is so important for making your audience remember what you've said. Once they've heard it again in the main body of your speech, and been hit by a powerful summary wrapping it all up at the end, even your most slow-witted listeners should know what you're on about.

It doesn't have to be subtle: 'telling them what you're going to tell them' can be as simple as saying, 'Tonight I'm going to be talking about . . .'.

The middle

We now come to the meat of your speech. There's a lot to think about in the middle section – the writing style that will work for you, and when and how you'll use quotes and make jokes. But first you need to decide how you're going to organise your material.

The way to structure the middle of your speech is to write out a few – ideally no more than three or four – of the main sub-themes of your subject. Try to put them in an order that makes for a clear and logical narrative. Then, by using clear signposting, you can signal to the audience when you have finished with one sub-theme and are embarking on another. Phrases that can help you here include 'turning now to . . .', 'let us now look at . . .', 'secondly', 'finally', 'so', 'nevertheless', 'as a result', etc. These words serve to mark transitions in your material, much as paragraphs and section headings do in printed text.

By demarcating the main body of your talk clearly like this, you break it down into manageable chunks. You make it easier for your audience to see where it is going, and the whole of your speech fits into a logical pattern, gracefully proceeding from point to point. The end of each chunk is a good place for a short and pithy phrase – a sound bite if you like – to sum up and move on.

Ever since the time of the ancient Greek and Roman writers, who analysed the art of rhetoric, three has been known as the magic number when it comes to writing speeches. For some unknown reason, people like hearing things in threes. As we shall see, the rule of three works on the small scale, with individual words and phrases. But it works on the large scale too, so if you want to have sub-themes in your speech, it helps if you can boil them down to three – 'There are three things I want to talk to you about tonight . . .'.

Mixing it up – repetition and variation

Repetition and variation are two of the most important features of a speech. Repetition helps to hammer your message home. But giving your speech variety, mixing up the rhythm, varying the language and injecting emotion in places – this all helps to keep your listeners on their toes. And by varying the rhythm, you can affect the way that your audience feels – you can convey a sense of excitement when you speed up, and of contemplation and consideration when you slow down.

How do you change the rhythm of your words? First, look at the length of your sentences and paragraphs. Of course, your listeners won't always know where your paragraphs begin and end – all they hear are words punctuated by pauses. But writing in paragraphs imposes a useful discipline on you as you're preparing the speech. Each paragraph should express one sub-theme of your argument, and you should aim to use each sentence within it to convey a single idea (in speechwriting especially, convoluted sentences with lots of sub-clauses generally don't work). As you look at the words on the page, then, you should be able to see how the rhythm of your speech will ebb and flow, as the length of your paragraphs and sentences changes.

The thing to remember, though, is that long sentences and paragraphs on the page don't usually mean that when you deliver your speech, you will slow down at that point. Most speakers speed up through long passages with lots of words in long sentences, for example when they are recounting anecdotes. But they pause at the end of each sentence. And they pause at the end of each paragraph.

So if you really want to slow things down for your audience, you have short paragraphs. And short sentences. Maybe really short.

Sometimes adding words can help to build up the pace, especially if they are words like 'so', 'therefore', 'in other words' or 'what this means is . . .', which help to tie sentences and paragraphs together and speed up the flow between them.

And do rhetorical questions help to slow things down? Indeed they do. They make you pause after them, to give your audience time to think about what you've just asked. Unusual turns of phrase also help to slow things down – you need to take care to say them properly, and your audience needs time to absorb what they mean. Practise reading your speech out loud, making a note of where you naturally tend to pause for breath: this will help you to control the rhythm of your words.

Generally then, if you want to cover a lot of ground quickly, speed up, using longer sentences and paragraphs. If you want to get people to focus on an idea, slow down. Short snappy phrases.

Clap-traps and laughter-traps

A good speech isn't a one-way street. Even before you take questions (if you do), your listeners have the chance to let you know what they think about your speech, and to some extent to participate in it. People like it when they feel that they're involved in a bit of a dialogue, rather than just being spoken at.

The most common forms of audience participation are laughter and applause. Asking for a show of hands is another good way of making your audience feel involved. Other less welcome forms of audience response include sitting in icy silence, and even giving you a slow hand-clap, booing you or whistling. Thankfully this kind of reaction is much rarer than laughter and applause.

Under normal circumstances, people laugh more readily when they're part of an audience than they do normally. There's something of a herd mentality at work, whereby one person finding a joke amusing can set everyone off (18th-century theatre managers understood this phenomenon well, and hired groups of people called 'claques' to sit in the audience and laugh and applaud in all the right places). Most people also would rather laugh than suffer the excruciating embarrassment of hearing a joke die on its feet.

The result is that you may find yourself being much funnier in your speech than you thought you were. And because you don't want to have to talk over laughter and risk any of your points being missed, it's a good idea to go through your speech and mark up anything which could conceivably raise a titter. At these points you'll be prepared – they may not cause much of a stir, but at least you'll be ready if your audience does laugh. You'll know that you may (with luck) need to wait for a couple of seconds before you move on to your next point.

Something similar applies to applause during a speech. Of course, speeches are much more likely to be applauded in some environments than in others. A strongly partisan audience (at a political conference, for example, or on other occasions when speakers are addressing their own people) may well clap whenever they have an opportunity, partly as a way of getting behind the speaker and participating in the speech. Again, it's an idea to mark up on your speaking notes the points where this might happen, so that you can be ready to pause for a few seconds.

Applause for a speech can, to a large extent, be manipulated. In fact, there's a long tradition of using devices to stimulate applause in an audience: these devices are called 'clap-traps'.

Of course, when you praise or thank someone, people may well clap afterwards. But you can also encourage your audience to applaud by giving them a sense of completion. This can involve a short sentence that logically concludes what has led up to it. It can involve a list, with the final item on it introduced with 'and finally' or something similar. Or it can involve a short, pithy sound bite which summarises the preceding argument in a memorable way. In each case, you're signalling the fact that one of the main sections of your speech has ended, and that you've just made one of your main points. Back this up with body language and tone of voice which also says 'Watch out folks, one of my main points is coming up', and your audience may well be primed to clap afterwards (if it's that kind of event).

One of the most famous examples of a clap-trap is from a speech given by Prime Minister Margaret Thatcher at the Conservative Party Conference in 1980. After arguing at length against carrying out a U-turn in policy, she summed up with two short sentences: 'You turn if you want to. The lady's not for turning.' Cue applause.

The most important clap-trap that you'll want to build into your speech comes at the end, where you need to signal well in advance that you're drawing to a close, but where you're no longer faced with the problem of having to continue talking once the rapturous applause dies down.

And finally – how to finish with a flourish

Every speaker wants their speech to finish, not just to stop: to end with a bang not a whimper, touching again on the handful of key points that have been made throughout the speech, 'telling them what you've told them', and drawing these points together in a few short, pithy, memorable sentences, before leaving the stage to thunderous applause.

It's a good idea to be thinking right from the start of the writing process about how you plan to end your speech, and how you'll use your structure to build up to it. You don't want it to be an afterthought. The conclusion of your speech is what you'll leave ringing in your audience's ears, and what will stay with them. If you're trying to change your listeners' minds, this is the time of maximum opportunity – when you've spelt out all your arguments, and shown as clearly and emotively as you can the direction that you want them to go in. If ever there's a moment where your audience members think 'Actually, maybe I will vote *x*' or 'In future, maybe I will do *y*, or join *z*', it needs to be now.

To help you finish strongly, you'll need to find a way of signalling to your audience when the time comes that you're drawing to a close, and of reinforcing in your audience's mind the central idea that you've been trying to communicate.

There are several different ways of making it clear that your speech is coming to an end. Probably the simplest is to be explicit, using phrases such as 'in conclusion', 'in closing', 'so to sum up', 'in this speech I've . . .' or 'let me end by saying . . .'.

At the same time, you can show that you are near the end by the manner of your delivery. Now is the time to slow down, and to start using shorter, more declarative statements that sum up your main argument, restating your main points in different words. You circle back with your closing remarks to where you began.

Often, ending powerfully means rounding off with a proposal, a resolution or a call to action. Here's a famous example of how to do it in style (from Lincoln's Gettysburg Address):

We here highly resolve that these dead shall not have died in vain – that this nation, under God, shall have a new birth of freedom – and that government of the people, by the people, for the people, shall not perish from the earth.

Ending with a quotation can be good too. Another very famous example (Martin Luther King):

And when this happens, when we allow freedom to ring, when we let it ring from every village and every hamlet, from every state and every city, we will be able to speed up that day when all of God's children, black men and white men, Jews and Gentiles, Protestants and Catholics, will be able to join hands and sing in the words of the old Negro spiritual, 'Free at last, free at last! Thank God Almighty, we are free at last!'

Finally, it helps to mark the very end of your speech with 'Thank you', just to signal that you really have finished. That's all folks.

> *A speech is like a love affair. Any fool can start it, but to end it requires considerable skill.* Lord Mansfield

3 Writing the speech

By now you should have a fair idea of the bare bones of your speech – the structure it's going to follow, the main subjects you'll be touching on, and the evidence you'll be putting forward to support what you have to say. But how are you going to put flesh on this skeleton – what, in other words, are the rules of good writing for speeches?

Ultimately the test of a speech, as of any form of communication, is whether it has the intended effect on the person who is on the receiving end. It sounds obvious, and yet it is extraordinary how often speakers fail to do the simple things that are necessary to reach their audience.

The reasons for bad writing

People write badly for all kinds of reasons, and these reasons aren't always to do with a lack of education. Academics are among the worst culprits when it comes to self-indulgent, wilfully obscure prose.

One of the commonest mistakes that people make with speeches, as with other kinds of writing, is to try too hard to sound impressive. It's tempting to use long, complicated words and sentences where a few short ones in plain English would do. This is bad enough in an essay, but it really doesn't work in something that's intended to be spoken.

It takes real confidence to say something in the clearest, simplest way that you can. It means that you're not hiding behind your language, but are doing your best to make your audience understand you. There's some risk in this, of course. If you present your arguments as clearly as you can, it makes it easier for people to scrutinise them, and maybe find a flaw in them. But it's a risk you have to take. The point of a speech isn't to show off how clever you are, but to get people to see things the same way that you do. And you won't do that by using obscure words, complicated phrases, and endless sentences full of twists and turns.

Even if you do want to show off how clever you are, you're still better off communicating as simply as you can. There are few people more impressive than those who know their subject so well that they can explain it clearly to someone who doesn't know anything about it. And there are few people so persuasive as those who believe in their own ideas so strongly that they want above all else to help everyone understand them.

In speechwriting in particular it can be tempting to fill your page with phrases that ultimately mean very little. These phrases may have all kinds of unnecessary double negatives and circumlocutions, but bounce along in their own way and come with their own kind of rhythm. It can be much more comforting to burble away, rather than work with the staccato sounds of things that have been said as plainly as they can be. More satisfying to say 'a not inconsiderable amount' rather than 'a lot', or 'in the final analysis I am of the opinion that' instead of 'I think'. But you need to resist the temptation.

Using simple, unpretentious language doesn't mean that you can't achieve soaring effects of rhetoric. In fact, in some ways it makes it easier to speak with real power, because it makes it easier to play with the speed and rhythm of your words. When Abraham Lincoln gave the Gettysburg Address, he used only 20 words of more than one or two syllables.

Another reason why people are sometimes tempted into bad writing is because they belong to a certain clique, which affects their choice of words. Many groups in society, whether it be doctors, lawyers, architects or teenagers, have their own specialised language. It can work as a badge of belonging – a particular jargon that people within the group understand, but not those outside it.

When you're one of the privileged insiders, the phrases you use can seem like just a convenient shorthand, allowing you to get your ideas across much quicker to those in the know. People on the 'inside' sometimes find it hard, though, to anticipate how alienating their use of specialised language might be to outsiders: how much it makes them sound as if they don't want to be understood by just anybody. And the trouble with jargon is that after a while you forget that it's jargon at all – you find yourself using it with people who haven't a clue what you're talking about.

Sometimes too, people are afraid to put anything of themselves into their speech, with the result that what they say comes across as stilted and uninteresting. Business people in particular are often reluctant to connect themselves personally to the ideas they're putting forward. They don't like talking about themselves, and yet providing first-hand accounts is what speeches are especially good for. Anecdotes, jokes, descriptions of lived experience: these are the things that work when you're standing in front of a live audience. You can't expect to be anonymous when you're standing at a podium, and you shouldn't try to be.

Writing and talking like a corporate robot can be very bad for your business. People connect with those who seem like real people, who show some individuality and even some vulnerability, and nowhere is this more true than in speeches.

Finally, there's good old-fashioned laziness. Why bother to think up your own turns of phrase when you can just lift someone else's? That's why hackneyed expressions and worn-out metaphors live on for so long. You don't have to pick out individual words to fit your meaning, or invent your own images to make your meaning clearer. All you have to do is string together a few collections of words that come ready-made for you.

You may not have a particular axe to grind (Benjamin Franklin) about not using clichés – you may not feel that originality should be the be-all and the end-all (William Shakespeare) of a speech. But try it at least some of the time. After all, variety is the spice of life (William Cowper).

Some rules for good writing

How do you make sure that your writing avoids all of the bad habits that you might otherwise fall into? In the 1940s the English writer George Orwell published a handy set of simple rules for good writing. They still apply today, and they can be adapted to provide some useful simple rules for writing for speeches.

Rules for good speechwriting

- First, never use a metaphor or other figure of speech that you are used to hearing or seeing in print – in other words, don't use clichés.

- Don't use a fancy long word when a short one will do just as well. In practice that often means preferring words that come from Anglo-Saxon ('think') to ones that come from Latin ('consider').

- Always cut words out if you can do so without it affecting your meaning.

- Always try to use the active voice ('the cat sat on the mat') rather than the passive ('the mat was sat on by the cat').

- And finally, don't use jargon, foreign words, old-fashioned phrases or scientific terms if there is an everyday modern English equivalent that will do just as well.

Of course, following these basic rules alone won't make you a great writer, but they should help you avoid being a really bad one.

Loaded language

Something else that you need to consider when you dress your ideas with words is that there is rarely a neutral way of doing it. Words come with implications and associations. They can be loaded. It's important to be aware of what that load might be, and whether it works for you or against you.

Even the way people talk about loaded language can be loaded. If they don't like someone else's loaded language they might call it 'spin', which has all kinds of negative connotations (not least the fact that it's what politicians do), and implies a heavily biased interpretation of things in the user's own favour. If they really dislike someone's loaded language, they might call it 'propaganda', which has even worse associations.

What's the difference between a 'plant' and a 'weed'? There's no botanical basis for the distinction – when someone calls a particular plant a weed, all they're really describing is their own attitude towards it – that for some reason they don't like it, or that it's in the wrong place. What's the difference between an organisation that is 'independent' and one that is 'unaccountable'? Between a 'freedom fighter' and a 'terrorist'? The difference is only what the speaker feels about the subject that they're describing.

Loaded language is often pejorative. But it can also be euphemistic, downplaying the seriousness of a situation, or making it sound less nasty than it really is. Armed forces around the globe are particularly good at this (or at least, they go in for it a lot) – 'friendly fire', 'ethnic cleansing' and 'collateral damage' have all become familiar.

Then there are the words with a positive spin, which are often used in ads to sell products, and by politicians to sell points of view. The aim is to bypass the rational mind and appeal directly to the wants and emotions of the listener, so that it might even seem absurd to argue logically against the speaker. Take 'tax relief', for example. Relief – you can almost feel the weight of that tax burden being lifted from your shoulders, can't you? Who in their right mind wouldn't be in favour of tax relief?

Loaded questions too, like loaded words and phrases, work by slipping the speaker's point of view into what might otherwise seem to be neutral language. They often take the form of presupposing things to be true when they haven't been proved. Take the classic 'When did you stop beating your wife?' – on the face of it this is a question about timing ('When . . . ?'), but it slips in a very provocative assumption.

Pollsters know all about this – that they can make a huge difference to the outcome of a poll by tweaking the language of the questions that people are asked. If they're trying to manipulate people in a certain way, a common technique is to spell out the implications of what they're asking, all in loaded language. If the question is 'Do you think there should be a referendum on the EU Treaty?', a certain number of people will agree. But probably not as many as if the question were 'Do you think we should have a say in how much control Brussels has over our lives?'

With all of these forms of loaded language, the question you need to ask in writing your speech is whether any bias in your words is so great as to be noticeable. All language comes with baggage, and everyone has their own point of view. But the most persuasive language colours its subject so subtly that it is practically undetectable. Think about the words you use carefully, and avoid anything that might appear to your audience to be overtly manipulative.

Language and discrimination

One of the most important ways that language can be loaded is in its descriptions of certain groups of people, and this is something that you have to be particularly careful about when you give a speech.

If you're talking about someone whose gender you don't know, don't assume that they're a 'he'. Many a speaker has alienated half of their audience by over-reliance on the male pronoun. To get round the problem you could keep saying 'he or she', but that's a little clumsy. Using 'we' a lot is good, when you can (but don't refer to yourself as 'we', unless you are a monarch). The gender-neutral 'they' can work just as well, and its informality shouldn't be a problem in a speech.

Be careful too about the tone of your remarks when you're talking about minority groups. You might not use any obviously discrimin-atory language in the way that you refer to a certain group, but if you're continually talking about 'them' and contrasting 'them' with 'us', you can create a very disquieting effect. With speeches in particular, it can be very easy to appear as if you're talking to a cosy, close-knit group, an 'us', to the exclusion of certain groups outside the auditorium. Even if they don't belong to those groups themselves, many of your listeners may feel uncomfortable if you do that.

Again, because it can be difficult to spot your own bias, it's a good idea to ask someone else to give your speech a quick read-through before you deliver it, and to be on the lookout for this.

Ultimately, writing speeches is about creating a kind of mood music, and if it is to work it has to work subtly. The words you choose need to do a number of things at the same time. You're getting across your argument, ideally as clearly as possible, without using jargon or showing off unnecessarily. At the same time, you're also conveying important information about *you* – the kind of person that you really are, and what you really think about things.

Whenever there's a conflict between what a speaker says and the way they say it, audiences have a tendency to believe the latter. The things you say apparently without realising it can seem more authentic than your carefully chosen message.

Writing for someone else

Writing a speech for someone else – perhaps the CEO of a company, or the head of a public-sector organisation – involves many of the elements that we've already looked at in this book. There are peculiarities to the process, however, which make it worth examining in its own right.

First, because the person you're writing for will generally be quite important, and their time therefore at a premium, it's part of your job to minimise their involvement in preparing and writing the speech. The typical process of writing for someone else involves a brief face-to-face meeting at the beginning, the production of a draft that goes back and forth a few times, and then sometimes a final short meeting to work on last-minute tweaks.

In order to minimise the demands on the speaker, you need to get a sense early on in the process, once you've researched the event and the likely audience, of who else in your organisation will be able to contribute to the speech. Ideally, in your initial face-to-face meeting with the speaker you'll talk mostly about the broad-brush things: the overall messages and the general approach of the speech. Much of the detail can usually be supplied by communications managers and subject specialists throughout your organisation.

Nevertheless, talking directly to the speaker at an early stage in the process is extremely important. First, you need to get a sense of how this person talks. And not just how they talk generally, but how they talk specifically about this subject, and in a relatively relaxed, conversational setting. It's a good idea to be scribbling away, and trying to catch verbatim the exact words that the speaker uses in describing the subject to you. This after all is very close to what you're aiming for with your speech: to make someone sound as natural and direct talking to a room full of people as they are talking to you, one-to-one.

It's also a good idea to listen out for the natural order in which the speaker approaches the subject, as they describe it to you. It's a curious fact, but when people talk out loud, they will usually order their material in the way that works best for a speech, and yet if you ask them to write their ideas down, you'll often get something that's not nearly as clear. For this reason, if you do need additional input from people around the place – policy officials, for example – it's always best to ring them up and ask them to explain it verbally, rather than giving you written material.

As the speaker talks to you about the subject of the speech, it's important that you contribute to the process. The speechwriter's job is to act as a catalyst, drawing out from the speaker content that can be used in the speech. That means asking apt questions, not only to test the main line of argument that the speech will be taking, but also to find out details such as how the speaker knows some of the other people who will be at the event. A face-to-face meeting is indispensable for drawing out some of the more personal, anecdotal material that works very well in speeches, especially at the beginning.

There now follows the process of drafting a speech outline for approval, and beginning to dress the skeleton with words that sound like the speaker's own. A good speechwriter fits their words precisely to the speaker, so that the speech sounds absolutely natural coming from them. That means knowing the speaker's mannerisms and characteristic turns of phrase. As you read your draft through, try to hear it spoken in that person's voice. You need to think about their pace (are they fast or slow?), their speaking style (do they tend to depart from the text?) and any peculiarities that they have when it comes to speaking, such as difficulty pronouncing certain words or letters.

When you write for someone else repeatedly, you get better each time you do it. It's important therefore to hear the speech when it is delivered, and to try to gauge the reactions of the audience. You will begin to develop a sense of what works and what doesn't with this particular speaker, and as time goes on you will begin to build up your knowledge of the kinds of anecdote that the speaker likes to recount, the lines of argument that they like to use and the jokes they like to tell. Over time your speeches for this person will become as good as, if not better than, anything they could have written themselves.

Writer's block and how to get round it

If you're struggling with any of this writing business, all is not lost. The tyranny of the blank computer screen may have taken over from that of the blank piece of paper, but many of the greatest writers throughout history have suffered from writer's block, and most professional speechwriters continue to suffer from it at some time or other. Fortunately, there are a number of ways round it.

For speeches especially, you can't beat a good natter to help you come up with ideas. A speech is like a conversation anyway, and most people think much quicker when they're speaking than when they're writing. Talking to someone about the subject of your speech can get your creative juices flowing. As we saw earlier, the process of explaining something out loud can help you to order the material for your speech in the most logical way. The brain likes dealing in stories, and having a chat can help you find the best one to link all the things that you want to say.

If you don't have someone who's prepared to act as a sounding board, it can still help to articulate your ideas out loud to yourself, as if you were indeed talking to someone else. Try not to do this in public, if you don't want people to stare at you.

Other good ways round writer's block include sleeping on the problem – you will often find the next morning that your brain has sorted out what you need to say. Distraction works too – go and do something else for a while, and try not to think about your speech at all. A change of scenery and some fresh air can work wonders.

If you're still struggling, you'll just have to make yourself write something – anything – on your subject, and forbid yourself from reading over what you've written until you've built up a decent amount of material. The important thing is not to edit yourself too early, and not to be too self-critical too soon.

4 Adding the flourishes

It's the little embellishments and grace notes that turn a workaday speech into something that really sings.

Humour in speeches

Humour isn't necessary for a great speech. Abraham Lincoln didn't exactly have them rolling in the aisles with the Gettysburg Address. Similarly a CEO talking to company employees behind closed doors, and telling them that they need to pull their socks up or the business will go under, might well dispense with the laughs. However, in the circumstances in which most people find themselves speaking in public – not on a momentous historical occasion, nor in front of an audience that they can browbeat – a few good jokes will be expected.

Using humour is also one of the most powerful persuasive techniques that exist, and it works in speeches for a whole number of reasons.

First, humour disarms an audience, making them more likely to be open to you and to your message. Humour puts people at their ease, and puts them in a good mood. And a comfortable audience is an audience with its guard down. An audience that is enjoying itself is less likely to over-analyse your speech. Getting a few laughs, especially early on in a speech, also helps you to relax as a speaker, and to come across more confidently.

A good joke or two can help to keep an audience's attention. People like laughing, and they'll be more likely to follow what you're saying if they think that there might be an enjoyable pay-off for them. Everyone's mind wanders from time to time when they are listening to a speaker – peppering your speech with humour helps to reel them back in with the prospect of something pleasurable.

Audiences like, and are drawn to, people who can make them laugh. Humour creates a sense of affinity between speaker and listeners, and when people feel that someone is fundamentally like them, they are more likely to accept that person's view of things. Nor is this sense of affinity necessarily false. If you can make someone laugh, and even more so if you can make a group of people laugh together at the same thing, it shows that you do indeed have a fairly sophisticated understanding of them.

Using humour can also be a good way of attacking your opponents without looking too mean. As Mark Twain said, 'Against the assault of laughter nothing can stand.' It's true – often the best way of countering an argument is not to dismantle it logically, but simply to laugh at it. And by laughing along with you, your audience is implicitly agreeing with what you're saying.

Humour works as a sign of goodwill on the part of the speaker – a sign that you're trying your best to give the audience what they want. In some more formal settings, such as when listening to a best man or an after-dinner speaker, a certain amount of entertainment is very much part of the deal for the audience. Even when it isn't, a few good jokes help your listeners feel that they are participating in the occasion, and are able, by laughing, to communicate something back to you about what you're saying.

Finally, and perhaps most importantly, associating your arguments with humour makes them more likely to be remembered by your audience. Even if they can't remember all the points you made, if you can make them laugh they'll remember you, and the warm feelings that they had about you and what you spoke about, long after everything else has faded.

There are any number of reasons, then, why humour is a powerful tool to use in speeches. But for these very reasons, there are rules that you should remember when you're trying to be funny in a speech.

Rules for jokes in speeches

The whole point about building rapport through humour is to show that you do in fact understand the people you're talking to. This means being careful to get your tone right, and to avoid anything that your listeners might possibly find offensive. It also means making your jokes relevant to them, and to the situation in which you're meeting them. What it does not mean is lifting a few old chestnuts out of a joke book and hoping that your audience will like them.

Where possible, you should also try to make sure that your jokes are relevant in the context in which you're using them. That means trying to make them blend in with the overall direction of your speech, without the join being obvious. Someone who tells a joke that is unconnected to anything else, and who signals well in advance that it is coming, is asking for it to fall flat on its face. More skilful speakers weave the humour into the narrative of a speech, so that they stake much less on the audience laughing at a particular joke. They also show greater virtuosity in finding material that is both funny and apt.

For the same reason, throwaway quips tend to work better than traditional gags with a set-up and punchline. Anecdotes work well too – stories taken from everyday life have the ring of truth, and such stories are already likely to have been adapted to a conversational style that is well suited to speeches. Don't start a joke or anecdote, though, by saying 'This is funny' or 'You will love this.'

Attributing an anecdote to someone else can also take the pressure off its need to be funny. A former cabinet minister used to tell a story about Neil Kinnock and what he said about mobile phones ('the only subject on which men boast about who's got the smallest'). If the audience laughed at that, fine. If not – well, it was Neil Kinnock's joke, not hers.

Finally, even if the function of your speech is primarily to entertain (as with a best man's speech at a wedding), it still helps to have an underlying narrative thread that connects everything together. This is what good stand-up comedians do: they tell stories that humour is an integral part of, giving you a sense of the world seen through their eyes; they don't just reel off a string of unconnected gags.

Ultimately it all comes down to judgement – about what's funny, and what's appropriate for your audience. In the end it's your call. But that in a way is the point: it's your judgement that you're demonstrating.

If they don't laugh ...

Even professional comics don't know if their humour will work until they try it – sometimes it does and sometimes it doesn't. And when you're giving a speech, you don't necessarily know how your jokes are being received. The fact that people don't laugh out loud doesn't mean that they're not amused by what you're saying.

The best thing to do when you're approaching one of the jokes in your speech is to be ready to pause after it, so as not to have to talk over the laugh it might get. But don't pause unless you have to. If there's no laugh, just carry on as if you never meant it to be a joke in the first place.

The very worst thing to do if people don't laugh at your jokes is to refer to the fact that they haven't. Leave that to 1970s comedians.

Rhetorical flourishes

One of the first people to write about classic tricks of rhetoric, Cicero, was said to have the sharpest tongue in Rome. He used it to gain high office, and to influence the policy of the Roman republic. But in the end he was decapitated, and his wicked tongue was cut out and stuck with pins. Spin doctors have never been popular.

The rule of three

No one quite knows why, but speakers have always found that by clumping things together in threes they can make them more appealing. As we've seen, it creates a pleasing effect on the big scale – speeches work well with three main sub-themes, for example. It works on the small scale too: grouping sentences and even words into patterns of three – technically known as 'rhythmic triads' – can make them more powerful.

One of the most famous spoken remarks of all time – Julius Caesar's *veni, vidi, vici*, 'I came, I saw, I conquered' – is about as good an example as you can get: the similarity of the three words makes them sound even more like a magic spell when they're spoken together. Most speeches contain at least one rhythmic triad, and some of them are very famous: 'government of the people, by the people, for the people' (Abraham Lincoln), 'never in the field of human conflict was so much owed, by so many, to so few' (Winston Churchill).

Matching pairs

In a similar way, arranging ideas in matching pairs can create an elegant sense of balance. They are especially useful for introducing ideas of contrast or comparison, and for emphasis, with the second word or phrase expanding on and developing the first: 'the survival and the success of liberty'.

Phrase reversal and antithesis

Another old trick in speeches is phrase reversal, as in John F. Kennedy's 'Ask not what your country can do for you – ask what you can do for your country.' Then there's antithesis, where you compare and contrast dissimilar elements: 'to friend and foe alike', 'give me liberty, or give me death', 'to some generations much is given. Of other generations much is expected'.

Repetition with variation

When you have a lot of different points to make, you can avoid using overly complex sentences by repeating certain words and using simple connecting phrases, so that your listeners concentrate in each case on the new term that is introduced.

This repetition with variation is a very old technique in speech-writing, and it can be used in a number of ways. The most familiar involves using the connecting phrase at the beginning of a number of clauses, as Winston Churchill famously did: 'We shall go on to the end, we shall fight in France, we shall fight on the seas and oceans, we shall fight with growing confidence and growing strength in the air, we shall defend our island, whatever the cost may be, we shall fight on the beaches, we shall fight on the landing grounds, we shall fight in the fields and in the streets, we shall fight in the hills; we shall never surrender.'

Most people know that Martin Luther King said 'I have a dream' in a speech. What is less well known is that in this speech he repeated 'I have a dream' ten times in a few minutes.

A similar effect can be achieved when the connecting word or phrase comes after each new thing that is introduced. Repetition of the same word or words at the beginning of successive clauses or sentences is known as 'anaphora'; when you repeat a phrase at the end it is called 'antistrophe'.

Occasionally, repeated phrases come both before and after, as in this famous example from Franklin D. Roosevelt: 'Here is one-third of a nation ill-nourished, ill-clad, ill-housed – NOW. Here are thousands upon thousands of farmers wondering whether next year's prices will meet their mortgage interest – NOW. Here are thousands upon thousands of men and women labouring for long hours in factories for inadequate pay – NOW.' This can be so powerful that your audience might even join in, and start chanting the 'NOW' with you.

Finally, here's something more recent, which also mixes things up with a repeated phrase: Barack Obama's speech after winning the Democratic presidential primary in South Carolina. 'Don't tell me we can't change. Yes, we can. Yes, we can change. Yes, we can. Yes, we can heal this nation. Yes, we can seize our future.'

Alliteration
Alliteration involves the repetition of the first sounds in a series of words, to create a striking effect, especially when they are spoken: 'the nattering nabobs of negativism' (Spiro Agnew).

Climax

When you're introducing a series of facts or ideas, you can create an increasingly impressive effect if you arrange them in ascending order of importance. The opposite effect – 'bathos' – involves creating a sense of anticlimax, and is best used only when you want to be funny.

Irony

Irony is the use of language which on the face of it means one thing, but in fact means precisely the opposite. It's quite a high-risk strategy in speeches – if it works, your audience will feel flattered that you credit them with enough intelligence to understand what you're really saying. The trouble is, conveying the fact that you're being ironic asks quite a lot of you as a speaker – you need to signal it through your tone of voice, but not make it too obvious. Irony is notoriously difficult to convey in writing, so there's also the danger that you'll deliver an ironic line completely 'straight' (you might want to mark it up in an eye-catching way in your speech notes). And in any given audience, there will be people who just don't get it, and they might come away with a seriously warped impression of what you stand for. It's best not to be ironic about anything too serious.

Imagery

Striking and original imagery is an excellent way of making your speech vivid. 'The Iron Curtain' is a well-worn phrase now, but it was new once, and introduced in a speech (by Winston Churchill). It's an excellent example of the way that good imagery works – it sums up a fairly complex idea in a single memorable phrase, and in a concrete way that appeals to the senses.

Simile and metaphor

Similes and metaphors are both forms of analogy, which work by comparing things that seem on the face of it to have little in common. Similes make clear the comparison, using such words and phrases as 'like' or 'in the same way as'; metaphors do without them. Metaphors jump right in and say that something *is* something else.

Mixed metaphors are often unintentionally funny – a famous example is 'the fascist octopus has sung its swan-song', which appeared in the Soviet propaganda sheet *Pravda*. Metaphors often work well, though, when they are extended: if the *Pravda* writers had just run with the fascist-as-octopus image, and pointed out a number of ways in which a fascist is like an octopus, they might have had better luck.

Plays on the familiar

This technique involves taking a well-known word or phrase and giving it a twist to make it memorable. 'A wolf in sheep's clothing' is familiar – calling Clement Attlee 'a sheep in sheep's clothing' earned Winston Churchill an entry in many dictionaries of quotations.

Sentence variation

As we've seen, mixing up the length of sentences is a useful way of controlling the pace of your speech. But sentence length is just one of the things you can vary: you can also alternate between sentences where the main clause comes at the end, and those where the main clause comes at the beginning.

Rhetorical questions

When you ask your audience a rhetorical question, you're trying to lead them to a conclusion that you already have in mind, and you may even answer the question yourself to make clear what that conclusion is.

Sentence fragments

Bold, declarative statements work well in speeches. Often, you can dispense with verbs, to make them even punchier. And speaking in sentence fragments encourages you to pause to let the facts sink in after each one. The following is an example (from a speech by David Cameron) of rhetorical questions and sentence fragments working together with repetition and variation.

Everyone knows that education, like our other public services, desperately needs radical reform. And who's the man standing in the way? Gordon Brown, the great roadblock.

Everyone knows that our economy needs lower and simpler taxes. Who's standing in the way? The great tax riser and complicator, Gordon Brown.

Everyone knows that business need deregulation to compete with China and India. Who's standing in the way? The great regulator and controller, Gordon Brown.

But - beware of big rhetoric

These, then, are some of the better-known rhetorical tricks and devices that are available to you as a speechwriter. But before you reach into the toolbox, a word of warning. High-flown rhetoric isn't fashionable these days. The old techniques still work, but they need to be understated. Use them sparingly, to give your own natural speaking style more clout when you need it. Your verbal flights will be more effective if they stand out against a background of simple, clear, conversational language. In the campaign for the White House, Barack Obama's overuse of smooth oratory became a target of attack: as Hillary Clinton said, 'You campaign in poetry, but you govern in prose.'

Writing for the ear - when to ditch what you learned at school

There are plenty of books around that provide transcripts of some of the classic speeches that have been made throughout history. Generally they read very well. But as you read them, remember that these aren't the speeches themselves, they're just records of them. The real speeches were delivered on particular days, to particular audiences (who sometimes – as in the case of Martin Luther King's 'I have a dream' – participated in the speech through their applause and shouts of encouragement and agreement), by particular speakers, each with their own distinctive voice.

A piece of written text can be read by anyone, but a speech is made to a particular group of people at a particular time. It's written for their ears and addresses their concerns. And it comes from an individual who is there in flesh and blood before them, not from a disembodied author. A speech therefore tends to be more personal in style than an essay or a magazine feature. Good speakers will often base what they have to say on their own personal experience, even when they are trying to make a wider point. And a speech is all about how words sound, not how they look on paper.

So when there's a clash between correct written English and what sounds natural when it comes from someone's mouth, the spoken word must win. Learning to write speeches means learning to write aloud, to write for the ear and not the eye. Even before you get to the rehearsal stage, you should be reading your words out as you write them, saying them aloud to see if they sound natural.

Reading out loud everything you write not only helps to refine the rhythm of your speech, but it can reveal hidden problems. Some lines look fine on paper, but are real tongue-twisters when you say them out loud. Some things can look completely innocent when they're written down, but sound very rude when they're spoken.

You should punctuate, too, according to the ear and not the eye. Punctuation should reflect the sound structure of the speech, reinforcing the rhythm and pace of your actual delivery. This also means punctuating for the lungs: give yourself time to breathe. If a sentence or paragraph sounds a bit breathless, it's probably too long. Break it up.

Some uses for bad grammar

Writing for the ear means capturing the way that people actually speak. That can mean using what some people would think of as bad grammar, such as sentences that start with 'but'. Sentences without verbs. Don't be worried if your computer underlines a lot of your sentences in green as you're writing them. Expressing yourself clearly is more important than good grammar.

In a similar way, throwing the odd bit of idiomatic language into your speech can be quite effective. When Norman Tebbit spoke about how his unemployed father in the 1930s had 'got on his bike' to find work, the allusion to the slang phrase 'on your bike' wasn't taken quite as he probably intended it, but it certainly gained attention.

Quote unquote - when, who and how to

Some speechwriters don't like putting quotations in speeches, as if they feel there's something a little underhand in using words that aren't their own. Certainly you don't want your text to be overburdened with quotations from other people. But used sparingly, as we'll see, quotes can work as a kind of celebrity endorsement of your argument. And they can add a poetic touch at key points, without the risk of ridicule for coining high-flown phrases yourself.

By all means quote, then, but not too often. Choose your quotes because the particular form of words they use expresses what you want to say better than you could say it. And if you're going to include a quote, it's often most effective to use it to sum up or round off a line of argument that you've already been pursuing, rather than dropping a quote in and then explaining what you mean by it. It helps if you either give the attribution of the quote or otherwise indicate in your delivery (by pausing briefly before it, for example) that you are quoting.

Someone who used quotes well in this way was Ronald Reagan, the Great Communicator himself. His eulogy following the *Challenger* disaster is a classic example: 'The crew of the space shuttle *Challenger* honoured us by the manner in which they lived their lives. We will never forget them, nor the last time we saw them, this morning, as they prepared for the journey and waved goodbye, and "slipped the surly bonds of earth" to "touch the face of God".'

5 Winning the argument

One of the most common reasons for giving a speech is to try to win the battle for hearts and minds. But how do you win over an audience that is neutral, or maybe even hostile, to what you have to say? How do you motivate people to act a certain way, to vote a certain way, or to buy a certain product?

The old declamatory, pulpit-bashing style of arguing has long gone the way of the dodo. Seeing old footage of politicians campaigning can be hilarious, with their overblown gestures and hammy tone of voice. But these were the styles that worked before microphones and big-screen projectors, when you had to make sure that the people at the back of the room would get the message.

Technology has brought about a big change in styles of oratory. One of the first to exploit the new media was US President Franklin D. Roosevelt, whose 'fireside chats' over the radio introduced a new, conversational tone. His calm, reassuring voice and homely language changed audiences' ideas of what speakers should sound like. Roosevelt could grandstand with the best of them when he wanted to, but through the radio he was coming into the homes of ordinary people, and you wouldn't start ranting and waving your arms about in someone's home.

These days you have to be subtle. People will be more open to persuasion if you talk to them as you would if you were having a conversation with them. Nobody buys the hard sell any more. By all means be passionate – people will think much more of the points you're making if you show that you believe them yourself, and really care about them. But you have to take people with you – you can't bully or cajole.

So in terms of delivery, things are different for speakers today than they were a hundred years ago. But fortunately, the techniques that make up a persuasive argument, which have been used since the time of the ancient Greeks, generally still work. Most are entirely respectable. A few are a little more dubious, logically and morally, but it's good to know what they are, in case someone tries them on you.

The gentle art of persuasion – by fair means

There's an old joke in which a traveller asks a local how he can get to such-and-such a place. 'I wouldn't start from here,' the local says. 'Start from over there – it's nearer.'

Perhaps the single most important rule in persuasion is that you have to start from where your audience are. If you start from a position that is too far removed from them, they'll simply stop listening to you.

Of course, there are a lot of things bound up in this. It means trying to understand what your audience members currently think, what they worry about, who they respect and who they don't, and what terms of reference mean something to them.

It means understanding what forms the basis of their belief systems – the fundamentals that they refer back to when they're thinking about a particular course of action. What are their current opinions founded on? Who or what do they accept as an authority? What are their values? The way you frame an argument might be different depending on whether you are speaking to a team of research scientists, for example, or to a church group. It also means understanding what you might have to offer your listeners, if they were to come around to your way of thinking.

This doesn't mean that you're pretending to your audience that you share their point of view when you don't. It just means that you under-stand it, and can show – through the language, analogies or references that you use – that you understand it. It means that you're walking with your audience through the steps that you want them to take, not calling to them from way off in the distance.

Finally and perhaps most importantly, starting from where your audience are means understanding what they *want*. This isn't just about appealing to crude self-interest. Most people want to feel good about themselves. They want to do what they think is the right thing. It's your job to persuade them what that right thing might be.

One of the most effective means of persuasion can be the first-person account: 'I used to think like this, until I realised *this*, or found *this* out, or had *this* experience.' You are saying to the audience, in effect, that you're asking them to go through a process of change that is similar to one you yourself have been through. Often, this involves trying to shift the very terms of the argument, to set the agenda in the way that *you* want it.

Establishing your credentials

One important way of giving your argument a boost is to establish your credentials for speaking on a theme, especially if they involve your having special insight or privileged access to knowledge in relation to your subject.

You might weave in anecdotes that on the face of it are about one thing, but which are implicitly saying 'Look, I've been working on this subject for a long time' or 'Look, I know some of the most important people in this area.' Try not to be too obvious in your showing-off, though.

Anticipating the counter-argument

In a formal debate, you know that other speakers will be arguing against you – your audience will hear both sides, and can make up their minds based on what they hear. With most speeches, though, the situation is more complicated than this. It's as if two lines of argument are going on at the same time, but only one of them is out loud. The other is going on in the mind of your audience, or rather in the mind of each individual audience member. They might be listening to you, but far from agreeing with you.

A classic way of dealing with resistance or objections in your audience is to anticipate the contrary argument to yours, and appear to let the two battle it out in your speech (letting your own favoured position emerge victorious, of course). If you go down this route, it's vital to represent your opponents' arguments fairly. As we'll see, many of the more dubious tactics used in persuasion centre on falsifying what the other side is saying. And, regardless of any moral objection to doing so, this can be risky. Nothing will turn your audience off quicker than the impression that you're misrepresenting the opposition's point of view.

So if you're arguing against a particular position, pay it respect. If you summarise what the opposition say, or what they offer, do so fairly. This means taking the trouble to consider and understand opinions that are different from yours. There aren't many points of view that are just plain stupid or evil, or at least many that you're likely to find yourself having to argue against. If your opponent's argument has some merit in it you should admit as much, before going on to say why you nevertheless don't agree with it. By understanding the opposition's case you'll raise your own game in arguing against it, improve the quality of the debate and, with any luck, sound more convincing.

At the same time, you don't want your audience to focus too much on the counter-argument. Your summing up of the opposition's case should be fair, but it should also be brief.

This is for two reasons. First, there is the danger that your opponent's argument will still linger on in your audience's mind, long after you've blown holes in it. It's like saying 'Don't think of a black cat' – even after you tell your audience that the black cat doesn't exist and that the very idea of a black cat is absurd, it may still be the black cat that they're thinking of half an hour later.

The second reason is that in any debate, it's always better to appear to be the one making the positive suggestions. Spending a long time picking your opponent's argument to pieces may be enjoyable, but it doesn't mean that yours is any better. There are usually more than two ways of looking at things, and the best way might be something that neither your opponent nor you have thought of.

It never helps to come across as a nay-sayer, finding fault with what other people think but not putting forward positive suggestions of your own. You can see this especially in politics – running a 'negative campaign' is not perceived to be a good thing. Far better to raise your opponent's argument fairly but briefly, send it packing equally quickly, and focus instead on your positive vision of how things ought to be.

Getting your facts right

How do you send your opponent's argument packing? Nothing beats a good fact, carefully chosen and powerfully rammed home. Of course, you need to make sure that your information is true, as far as you can ascertain. Check any statistic carefully before you mention it. You don't need to name your source in the speech itself, but make sure you know where your figures come from in case someone challenges them.

Statistics are dry, though, so you need to work to make them speak. You need to unpack their implications, and bring them home to your audience in ways that will mean something to them. You need to put them in human terms, make analogies out of them, use them in anecdotes. Examples are always more persuasive than numbers alone – use anything that will create concrete images in the mind of your audience.

Say you were arguing against the idea that health and safety legislation imposed an intolerable burden on businesses, and made them uncompetitive. You could go to a respected source and find out how many people were seriously hurt at work in a given year. A nice fact, which works in your favour. But don't just let it hang there: follow it up. You might say, 'That's the equivalent of one every . . . seconds.' You could point out how many that added up to since you started speaking. You could even give a few examples of individual stories that lie behind the bare figures, giving a human face to the statistics. These are all ways of following up your fact creatively.

It's a curious fact about statistics that some ways of presenting them are much easier to grasp than others. Suppose you're talking about something that happens fairly regularly, and you want to emphasise its importance by bringing home to your audience just how frequent it is. You could say that something happens 36,500 times a year, or (which is pretty much the same thing) four times every hour. But it is much more effective either to talk about the frequency of a single occurrence ('once every 15 minutes') or to go for a nice round number ('100 times a day'). These figures are all roughly equivalent, but some are more memorable, and will have greater impact, than others.

Another thing about statistics is that people are wary of them. There are 'lies, damn lies and statistics', as somebody once said. That's why when you're introducing them, it's usually best not to use the word 'statistic' at all. 'Statistics show ...' sounds boring at best, suspect at worst. And don't say 'research indicates', or 'experts have shown'. You should just say, in effect, 'such-and-such is the case'. Or 'the truth is x', or 'the fact is y'. If you're really confident about your fact, you can signal to your audience that it's coming, and make it stand out: 'You know, you often hear people say such-and-such. But the truth is quite the opposite. Did you know that ... ?'

It can also help to make a statistic more compelling by relating it directly to your speech, and by weaving a little story around it. To say, for example, 'I did some research for this talk, and I found out that ...' is more subtly persuasive than just introducing a bare fact.

How your facts might be attacked

Before you put too much weight on certain types of evidence in your speech, it's a good idea to consider how a sceptical or hostile listener might attack them by asking an awkward question.

You might give a figure as an average, for example. But what sort of average are you talking about? Is it the mean (where you add a number of values up, then divide by the number of values), the median (the middle value when they are arranged in numerical order) or the mode (the value that occurs most frequently in a given sequence)?

Depending on what you're talking about, these different ways of determining an average can produce very different results.

Similarly, you might base your argument on information from a survey. Hard evidence, it might seem. But what if the number of people interviewed was so small as to make the results of your survey statistically insignificant? Or what if there was some hidden bias in the way that participants were selected, or in the questions that they were asked?

Graphs and diagrams are also very easy to manipulate to give a misleading impression. Fluctuations in a share price can be made to look more extreme, for example, if the values along the y (or vertical) axis don't start at 0, but at a higher number.

Endorsement

Advertisers have long known how effective it is to use celebrity endorsement to help sell a product. The same is true of speeches, and whatever point of view you're trying to get across to your audience.

We've looked at what makes a good quote for a speech. But for the purposes of winning an argument, it's worth remembering that a well-chosen quote is one of the best weapons in your armoury. It's as if you're saying, 'Don't just take my word for it – this is what so-and-so said about it.' And the advantage of using quotations as implicit endorsements is that the quotes you find (in specialised dictionaries of quotations grouped by subject, or on the web) are likely to be pithy, and have already shown that they have something memorable about them.

There are a few pitfalls that you will need to avoid, though, if you want to try to win an argument by showing that prominent figures in the past have agreed with you. The first is the danger that you will misjudge the regard that your audience have for the person you're quoting. This is where the research you do on your audience will be invaluable. Who do they see as an authority? Whose endorsement are they likely to value? It's no good quoting somebody if your audience hate them.

Second, you need to make sure that you don't misrepresent what your famous predecessor actually said. You have to get your quotation absolutely word for word (and beware, on the web these days there are all kinds of dubious, badly spelt, and grammatically suspect versions of famous quotes floating about – make sure that yours comes from a reputable source, ideally corroborated by another one). There's something about quotations from speeches that makes them particularly prone to being tinkered with when they're retold. 'Blood, sweat and tears', 'you've never had it so good', 'rivers of blood' – these are all famous phrases from speeches, attributed to British politicians, and all of them are misquotes.

Just as importantly, you need to make sure that the context in which a quotation was originally used also supports your use of it. If your audience know the person you're quoting well enough to be impressed by the fact that you're quoting them, they may also know their words well enough to know if you're taking them out of context, and they won't like it if you do.

Finally, you have to avoid any suggestion that you're name-dropping just for the sake of it. Even if you're talking to the John F. Kennedy appreciation society, it's not enough just to throw in a few quotations by John F. Kennedy. Celebrity quotations work when they are relevant to a particular audience, but only if the words are also relevant to the particular issue that you're talking about. The quotation itself needs to work in the context in which you're using it, regardless of who it is you're quoting. Audiences are very sensitive to attempts by speakers to ingratiate themselves by pretending to be part of a community that they don't in fact belong to.

In praise of the sound bite

Sound bites have a bad press: coming out of the mouths of politicians in 10-second news clips, they can seem to embody everything that's bad about modern public life – they can appear to be glib, smug, a triumph of style over substance.

Used as part of a longer argument, though, a good sound bite can work wonders. In a few well-chosen words, you can sum up the logic of what you're saying in a pithy, memorable way. Think of it as the clincher, the climax that your argument has been building up to.

Appealing to your audience's better nature

Another classic strategy in arguing your point is to appeal to your audience's better nature. Sometimes this can be an appeal to reasonableness – 'Surely we can agree to put aside our differences on this, and work together?' Sometimes it involves appealing to an implicit shared self-image, since most people like to think of themselves as doing the right thing – 'Can we, as a nation, allow this to happen?' Sometimes it involves invoking an explicit set of principles that the audience have notionally signed up to already, and holding them to account in relation to it. A classic example comes from Martin Luther King's most famous speech: 'I have a dream that one day this nation will rise up and live out the true meaning of its creed: "We hold these truths to be self-evident, that all men are created equal."'

Logic versus emotion

There are many different types of evidence that you can use to try to persuade your audience of something, and most good speeches won't rely on any single one of them, but will use a number in combination. However, logic can only get you so far in winning an argument. The greatest speakers throughout history have realised that logic can be a poor match for emotion in a speech. The point about many of the classic tricks of rhetoric is that they make your speech more emotive, which for most audiences means also making it more persuasive.

Winning the argument - by foul means

The dark arts of dubious argument have been around for a long time, too. It's not a good idea to try to use them yourself, but you should be aware of what they are, in case you find yourself on the receiving end.

Ad hominem arguments

The speech equivalent of 'playing the man, not the ball'. When an argument is *ad hominem* (the phrase means 'to the man' in Latin), instead of attacking an idea on its own terms, you go for the person who argues in favour of it, casting doubt on their honesty, for example.

Motherhood and apple pie

'Motherhood and apple pie' refers to value statements and loaded terms that seem bold on the face of it, but which just about everybody is likely to agree with anyway. Motherhood and apple pie statements are a form of truism or platitude, and are generally used by speakers to inveigle themselves into an audience's good books.

A politician, for example, might stand up and say that they 'believe in freedom'. But who would say that they didn't? Freedom, most people would agree, is a good thing. Saying that you believe in it doesn't tell your audience anything – whose freedom are you talking about? Freedom from what, or freedom to do what? People's interpretations of freedom differ greatly, so you need to do more than just say you believe in it for your statement to have any substance.

Switching the question

'People ask "Can we afford to have Trident?" But I say, "Can we afford *not* to have Trident?"' This is a glib way of avoiding an awkward question.

Begging the question

Begging the question is one of the more sly tricks of rhetoric, and often involves slipping an assumption or implication into your argument, without backing it up or providing any proof for what you claim. You might say, for example, 'Can we afford five more years of Labour lies?' But what evidence are you giving that Labour have lied?

Circular arguments

Circular arguments go round and round, unsupported by anything outside themselves. For example:

'How do we know that God exists?'
'Because the Bible says so.'
'But how do we know that the Bible is right?'
'Because it is the word of God.'

Either-or arguments

'Either you're with us or you're with the terrorists.' Presenting stark alternatives, either-or, is usually both logically dubious (things are rarely as clear-cut as this) and provocative – most listeners will resent attempts to force a position on them in this way.

The straw man

A straw man argument involves attacking a caricature or misrepresentation of your opponent's position, rather than the real one. It comes from the 'straw men' that army recruits practise their bayonet skills on – they look like the enemy, but they're a lot easier to hit, and they don't fight back. So 'setting up a straw man' involves attributing a point of view to your opponent that superficially resembles their actual point of view, but is easier to refute. Often it involves overstating the other person's position.

Your opponent might say, for example, 'I think we should relax the laws on cannabis.' Setting up your straw man to stab, you might respond – 'No. Allowing unrestricted access to drugs would destroy the very fabric of society.' But your opponent hasn't been talking about allowing unrestricted access, just about relaxing laws. And they haven't been talking about drugs generally, but about one specific drug.

False analogy and false inference

Analogy involves showing the similarities between (usually two) ideas, objects or events. With false analogy and false inference, though, you use the similarities between the things you're comparing to imply that they share other properties, when in fact they don't, or you imply a logical or causal link between two things that have something in common, when there isn't necessarily a link. For example: 'The universe works like the mechanism of an intricate watch. A watch is made by a watchmaker. Therefore the universe must have been designed by an intelligent creator.'

Exceptions to the rule

'My granddad smoked a packet a day, and he lived to be 90.' Your granddad might just have been very lucky. And he might have lived to 100 if he hadn't smoked.

Guilt by association

Guilt by association is a type of *ad hominem* argument, in which you attack someone's position not on its own terms, but by associating it with bad things or bad people. A common form of guilt by association involves 'playing the Hitler card', for example: 'Hitler supported euthanasia, therefore euthanasia is wrong.'

Reductio ad absurdum

Reductio ad absurdum, or reducing something to the absurd, involves taking an argument to bizarre lengths, to try to undermine it. You might argue against allowing free movement within the EU, by working out what would happen if every person in every EU member state decided to come to the UK at the same time. In practice that's not likely to happen.

6 Editing and rehearsing your speech

With luck, by this stage you should be feeling pretty pleased with yourself. You've found out all about your audience and the event you're speaking at. You've worked out exactly what you want to get from your speech. You've structured your material to make it easy to follow, from an engaging start, via a middle section that covers everything you want to say but with interesting changes of pace, through to a rousing conclusion.

Above all, you have a draft. At this moment, you might feel that these hard-won pages of text are pretty precious to you. Unfortunately, you're going to have to manhandle them, chop them down and push them around, before you have your finished speech.

You need to make sure that the draft you've got does the job that you originally intended it to do. It's easy in the early stages of drafting to let your writing run away with you, with the result that your speech gets out of shape. Now's the time to rein yourself in, and separate the happy turns of phrase that you've hit upon from the bits that just don't work. Culling all but the best examples or anecdotes is a key to being brief, which most good speeches are. Throughout the editing process, you need to keep asking: 'What exactly am I trying to say here?' and 'Have I said it well enough for my audience to understand me?'

Cutting it down and fleshing it out

The first thing you need to do is to read through your speech quite quickly, and get an idea of its overall structure and rhythm. Are there parts where the pace dips? Have you spent a lot of words on things that aren't really important, or skipped over things that you really want your audience to notice? A good speech is all about balance, and as you read through what you've written and compare it with what you originally set out to achieve, you'll probably want to make some changes of emphasis.

How do you do this? First, by cutting out anything that's redundant to the point you're trying to make.

> *Let thy speech be short, comprehending much in few words.*
> Ecclesiastes

This might mean getting rid of whole sentences in passages which are too flabby. And as you read through line by line, you'll nearly always find unnecessary words here and there. By removing them, not only will you be able to give more emphasis to the points that really matter, but your language as a whole will become tighter.

It might also mean adding material in important areas, and breaking your words up into shorter paragraphs and sentences, so that the pace of the speech slows at these important points.

Look next at your argument. Put yourself in the position of someone who isn't familiar with it (or ideally, ask such a person to read it through). Are there any points in your speech where they're likely to get lost? Any references or allusions that mean something to you, but which your listeners might need to have explained? Are there any jumps in the argument that need elaborating because you've left things implicit, or are there places where you have contradicted yourself?

If there's the slightest chance that what you're saying could be controversial, it's a good idea to give your speech draft what's called a 'defensive read-through'. You know what you mean to say, but are there things in your text that could be misinterpreted? Some of the most famous speech quotes in history have been taken out of context, making them say something different to what was intended by the original speaker. You don't want to be remembered for saying something you didn't mean.

So put yourself in your most mean-minded, uncharitable frame of mind, and give your speech a final reading. Has the speech left you any space to misconstrue it? Are there any lines which, taken out of context, would make it sound as if you were saying something that you actually aren't? Mark these points as you read your speech through, and adjust them so that even the most hostile member of your audience has nothing to get hold of.

Look now for anything that might be seen as cliché or jargon, and cut it out. No 'impact' used as a verb, no 'blue-sky thinking', no 'thinking outside the box . . .'. Look for any acronyms that your audience might not be familiar with, and make sure you spell them out the first time you use them.

Look for any way of making your language clearer and simpler. Cut out any repetition, except for emphasis. Delete any words that don't add anything – do you really want to say 'I was really quite surprised'; couldn't you just say 'I was surprised'? Get rid of any verbal tics that could distract the listener, anything that sounds trite and, in general, any language that isn't appropriate for the audience and the occasion.

Look for any mistakes you might have made in grammar or usage. If you don't know whether you mean 'infer' or 'imply', consult a dictionary. Finally, look at the statistics or quotes that you're planning to use, and check that you've got them right.

Practice makes perfect

Speaking in public is a skill, and as with any skill, you get better with practice. There's no substitute for it. And just like a footballer or a soldier, you practise partly so that when you are in a highly stressful situation you will do the right thing without needing to think about it.

Rehearsal is the final stage of fine-tuning your speech – the last chance you have to weed out the jokes that don't quite work, the phrases that sound odd when you say them out loud, and the long-winded descriptions that could be shortened. Rehearsal also helps you get used to speaking alongside your visual aids, if you're using them.

When you rehearse, try to recreate as closely as you can the conditions that you'll encounter on the big day. If you're going to be standing up, stand up. However embarrassing it may seem, try to rehearse using your normal speaking voice. Speak at the pace that you will on the day, and get used to reading the whole thing through, without going back and starting sections again.

Part of the trick of becoming a better public speaker is to make yourself do things that most people normally find uncomfortable. Make a tape recording of your speech, and play it back. This is a process that is likely to have you squirming. Most people sound strange to themselves when they hear a recording of their voice, but you can use this phenomenon to detach yourself from your speech, and put yourself in the position of your listeners.

If you can, listen to the tape of your speech all the way through, as if you were sitting in the audience. As with your first read-through, think about the big things. Do you give the right amount of weight to the different sections of your speech? Does the argument flow? Are there changes of rhythm and tone to keep you interested? Above all, what general impressions does your speech leave you with, and how do these compare with the fundamental aims that you first identified for your speech? Make a note of these overall impressions. Keep careful track of the time, too. As delivered, does the speech come in under or over your allotted time?

Another uncomfortable but useful experience is seeing what you look like while you speak. If you have access to a video camera, use that; otherwise, try to watch yourself in a mirror as you rehearse. Do you have any distracting or irritating physical tics as you talk? Do you fidget? Do you slouch? Do you look shifty? As you rehearse, try to slow your movements down, and to be still. Still people look more confident, and confident people are more persuasive. Practice holding a steady gaze, and make your gestures deliberate, backing up the message of your words.

Perhaps most uncomfortable of all, but certainly most useful, is to rehearse your speech in front of someone you can trust, who can be brutally honest about what works and what doesn't. It helps if this person isn't already familiar with what you'll be discussing. You may feel like throttling this person at the time, as they pick apart the words you've worked so hard on, and fail to understand what seems perfectly obvious to you. But you'll thank them later.

Based on what these various rehearsals reveal, you'll be able to fine-tune your speech, making changes of emphasis to hone your overall message, clarifying points that might confuse your listeners, cutting the text down to fit the time it takes to deliver it, and expanding on important sections if you have any time left over.

You're now ready to start preparing the notes that you'll take with you into the arena.

Preparing your notes

As we've seen, there are arguments both for speaking from the full text of a speech, and for using pared-down notes with only the most important bits spelt out in full. Once you have the final version of your speech all worked out, you'll need to think about the physical form that your speaking notes will take.

Preparing your notes carefully can mean, paradoxically, that you sound as if you're not relying on notes at all. Variations in pace and tone not only help you to keep your audience's attention, but they also bring you closer to the rhythms of a voice in normal conversation, making your speech sound more off-the-cuff, and therefore more sincere.

By marking up your text or your notes, you can build these variations into your speech. Someone who knew all about this was Charles Dickens, who read from his work in front of large audiences, and who was one of the most effective public speakers there has ever been. His speaking notes still survive: next to the text that he read out, there are all kinds of scribbles for his own benefit, reminding him of what was coming up, and telling him to quicken or slow the pace, or change his tone of voice, accordingly.

In a similar way, you may find it helpful to mark in advance where a pause might help to focus the audience's attention, or where you might want to start building up to a major point, or to your conclusion. If you think there is any danger of you reading out these notes to yourself (and it does happen . . .), print out the text of your speech and add your notes-to-self in handwriting.

If, having rehearsed your speech and timed your delivery, you think that you might overrun, you can mark up in your notes the sections that you can skip if you need to. This ensures that your overall message won't get lost if you're hurried.

If you're using shortened speaking notes, it helps if one of your cards or pieces of paper has an overview of the entire speech, with some of the main headings, which can serve as a map in case you get lost. Brief mnemonics can remind you, in a few words, of anecdotes or lines of argument that would take up a lot of space if you wrote them out in full.

Use a font size that is big enough for you to read without having to squint (and using bold type and double spacing can help prevent you getting lost in a dense mass of words). Number your sheets clearly, in case they get shuffled (as you finish reading from one, move it to the back of the pack). Try not to have a page break in the middle of a section: you don't want to have to pause halfway through giving a quote or making an important point while you turn the page.

Use thick paper or card for your speech text or notes – thin paper can easily get torn. And bear in mind that your notes themselves will form an important part of your presentation: your audience will be curious about them, and if they appear dog-eared, crumpled or dirty this will reflect badly on you as a speaker.

Finally, whether you're using full text or shorter notes, if you're planning on using visual aids you need to mark the points where you'll be introducing each slide or illustration.

Preparing your visuals

If you do decide to use slides, try to keep them simple. Ideally, restrict yourself to one main idea per slide, and include nothing that's not relevant. We've all seen PowerPoint slides that look like pages of a book, and heard people who speak straight from their slides. It's not a pleasant experience.

Keep the text on the slide down to a minimum: if there's any explaining to be done, do it in your speech. Make sure it's all big enough to be legible at the back of the room. And try not to get carried away – be sparing with the number of slides you use, and use them only for those things that would be difficult to explain verbally.

Finally, rather than having slides that simply repeat what you're saying, think about using your images more creatively. You could have slides with one-liners on them, for example, which make a provocative statement or raise a question that is relevant to a particular point in your speech, but which you don't refer to explicitly at all. Or you could have slides without words, instead showing images that somehow relate to what you're saying. This can be a more oblique and interesting way of using slides, developing a dialogue between your images and your speech, rather than creating competition between them.

7 On the day

The Romans used to think that it was a good idea for speakers to hold in their urine in the hours leading up to a big speech, to guarantee that they spoke with a real sense of urgency. In more recent times this idea has fallen out of favour.

Dealing with nerves

Everyone gets nervous when they speak in public. Some of the greatest orators in history have suffered terribly before taking to the podium: John F. Kennedy was often sick with nerves before he gave a speech. If you're getting pre-speech butterflies, console yourself with the thought that you're in good company. Remember too that while feeling nervous is largely out of your control, how you deal with it is very much up to you.

Listen to some relaxing music, or distract yourself by chatting to the event organisers or to other speakers. Breathe deeply, and try to relax the muscles in your neck and shoulders especially. Relax the muscles in your face by opening your mouth wide, and exaggeratedly grinning and looking surprised. Try to do this where no one can see you.

Warm up your vocal cords by reading aloud something from the paper, and lubricate them by sipping some water. Avoid caffeine – you don't want to come across as jittery. Don't touch the hard stuff – alcohol and public speaking don't mix. Save it for when you've sat down.

Be ready to pause for a moment before you start speaking. It gives you a chance to collect yourself, and it makes people pay attention.

Remember that people rarely come across as nervous as they feel. You might think it's obvious that you're absolutely terrified, but your audience probably won't spot it. And even if they do spot it, there are far worse crimes than sounding nervous when you give a speech. Don't worry if you're quaking in your boots at the thought of talking to all those people, but don't refer to it either. Your audience will understand if you sound nervous, but talking about it will only distract them and make them feel awkward. Soldier on and do the best you can to sound confident.

Arranging the venue

The venue can have a major effect on the presentation of your speech. If you have some say over the kind of place where you will speak, it can become an important part of your message. US President Ronald Reagan gave his most famous speech attacking the Soviet Union standing in front of the Berlin Wall. The head of a company might speak at a sporting venue if they want to encourage their workers to improve their performance (it's corny, but it's done).

Even if you can't choose the venue (and for most people that won't be an option), there may still be things you can do to affect the way that the space is laid out, to help you make the most of your presentation.

Pay particular attention to the backdrop that you'll be speaking in front of. Make sure that there's nothing behind you that will compete for your audience's attention – a window, say, or (worst of all) other audience members. In any audience there may be those who are fidgeting with boredom, or who look like they're about to nod off – at least if they're all facing the same way that shouldn't be obvious to anyone except you, the speaker.

Encourage the event organisers to leave as little distance as possible between you and your audience. It's easier to build up a sense of intimacy, and to get audience members to laugh or applaud, if you're all close together. Your listeners can see your facial expressions, and hear what you're saying without you having to project your voice. They may also pay more attention if they feel that they're under your watchful eye.

Finally, see if a clock can be put somewhere in your line of sight as you speak, so that you can keep an eye on the time without making it obvious.

Presentation

When you speak in public, you need to remember that you are part of your message. Even before you've opened your mouth, your audience will be paying attention to the way you dress and how you hold yourself. Then when you do speak, they'll notice your tone of voice and the gestures you make. For good or bad, this will all affect how they receive what you actually say, reinforcing it or undermining it.

However good a job you've done in writing your speech, when you come to deliver it many of the most important cues that your audience will receive are non-verbal. You need to make sure that everything about the way you look and sound reinforces what you want to say.

Dress

Of course, you need to make an effort with your appearance when you're giving a speech. But what exactly does that mean? How should you dress, to help your speech get the most favourable response?

You'll need to wear something that you feel comfortable in. But above all, you want your style of attire to convey authority. With very few exceptions (Richard Branson and Bill Gates, for example, wear their more casual style almost as a badge of honour), that means dressing at least a little more smartly than your audience. You are the one everyone will be looking at. Exactly how you do it is up to you, but dressing smartly shows a fundamental respect for your audience and for the event at which you're speaking. It also shows that you respect yourself. All of this is intended to convey the message 'I'm someone who is worth listening to.'

Body language

A confident style of speaking means a number of things. Physically, it means taking up the space you have. If you're speaking from a stage, walk onto it purposefully. If you're just standing up to speak, stand up straight. If you can move about, stretch your legs and do so. If you have to speak from a lectern, don't hide behind it. If you're just standing there, try to look comfortable, as you rehearsed – no shuffling or fidgeting.

Eye contact: who are you looking at?

Eye contact helps to hold the audience's attention, and it works even for those members of the audience you don't look at directly. They can see that you're holding the gaze of *someone* not too far from them, and it's still engaging. A good trick is to pick out a few individuals around the room – one to the left, one in the centre, one to the right – and use them as fixed points that your gaze can return to. Not only does this make you scan the whole of your audience, but it can help you keep a conversational tone in your voice, as if you were really just talking to one audience member at a time.

Your voice

Finally, there's your voice itself. Confident speakers speak clearly, towards the lower end of their natural range, and they project their voice. But they don't shout. In fact, as long as people at the back can still hear you, a relatively quiet tone can be surprisingly effective, conveying a sense of calm and assurance.

Queen Victoria used to say of Prime Minister William Gladstone, 'He speaks to me as if I were a public meeting.' Even when you *are* addressing a public meeting, it can still be a good idea not to sound as if you are. A conversational tone often works best, even when you're talking to 500 people at once. Try to speak in a way that is natural, direct, low-key, casual. This puts listeners at ease, and creates a sense of community between audience and speaker.

It's important too that you avoid any risk of sounding patronising or arrogant. A little humility in a public speaker never goes amiss, and that means not sounding as if you're lecturing your audience. By speaking to your listeners in a respectful tone right from the beginning, you make it much more likely that they will be swayed by what you have to say.

Lastly, try not to let your nerves make you go too fast. Speak at the pace you practised in rehearsals. Breathe regularly and deeply. And don't be afraid to pause, either to emphasise an important point or to give yourself time to catch your breath.

The power of confidence

What all these things convey is that you yourself have confidence in the value of what you're saying, and in your own right to be claiming these people's attention. It's very basic, nature-documentary stuff. You're not trying to be domineering, but through your body language, you're claiming the right to a hearing. You're not apologising for being there. You have something to say that's worth listening to.

There can be a terrible circularity to body language and public speaking. Look as if you expect your audience to pay attention to you, and they'll probably do that. Look as if you expect to be ignored, and they'll probably do that too.

Finally, rather than trying to feign all the different physical and verbal signs of being confident, it's a lot easier if you can convince yourself that you *do* have something worth saying, so that your confidence is genuine. You can help to build this confidence by making sure throughout the writing process that you are true to yourself, and that what you say is robust – the first step in persuading somebody of something is to believe in it yourself.

Speaking with visual aids

There's a knack to using visual aids as you speak, and most of it involves trying to avoid being upstaged by your silent sidekick. All the time that your visuals are on display, you're fighting a battle with them for your audience's attention. Make sure they don't get the upper hand. If you keep your slides few and simple, your audience's attention will wander every time you bring up a new one, but then it will come back as you explain what it all means. Keep it that way. When you bring up a new slide, try to avoid turning your back on your audience to look at it. Pause before you carry on speaking. And when you've shown the last slide that you're going to use, by all means turn the projector off completely.

Is this thing on? Using microphones

Some very experienced speakers have got into trouble with microphones that they didn't realise were on. At the end of a G8 session in St Petersburg in 2006, President George W. Bush greeted Prime Minister Tony Blair with 'Yo, Blair. How ya doin'?' He went on to talk at length, with four-letter frankness, about problems in the Middle East, all gleefully reported in the papers the next day. The transcript ends with Tony Blair tapping the microphone and saying, 'Is this . . . ?' Yes, it was.

The safest course is never to say anything when there are microphones around that you wouldn't want broadcast to your entire audience. Not even under your breath. Modern microphones are more sensitive than most people's hearing, so they can pick up quieter things than you'd register in normal conversation. And just because you can't hear your words coming out through a public address system, it doesn't mean that your microphone isn't on.

Don't assume either that you have to use a microphone that has been laid on for you. If you have a reasonably strong, clear voice, you may come across better without amplification. If you want to look sincere, in particular, it can help to stand before your audience with as few technical accoutrements as possible.

If you do decide to use a microphone, and it is hand-held or fixed to your lectern, make sure you don't get too close to it: most speeches aren't improved by being accompanied by the sounds of heavy breathing. About ten inches away from the mike should do it. A good rule of thumb is to see whether you are 'popping your Ps': when you say words with plosives in them – 'Ps' and 'Ts' especially – is your microphone registering a little percussive bang, as it's hit by the shock wave of air coming from your mouth? If it is, you're too close.

If you're planning on roaming around the stage and using your hands a lot, you might opt for a clip-on mike with a small portable receiver – check first that there's one that you can use comfortably.

Dealing with the unexpected

It happens: despite all your best efforts in preparing your speech, something unexpected intervenes. The PA system packs up. The lights go off. The event overruns so badly that you have to cut your speech by five minutes.

All you can do is to prepare your speech in such a way that it does not *depend* on technology – as we've seen, the best use of visuals in any case is as an add-on, rather than as something indispensable. In all but the largest venues, you can make up for a faulty PA system by projecting your voice. And when you prepare your notes, you can mark up those sections that can be jettisoned in an emergency, without too much loss to the whole.

Should misadventure befall you, acknowledge it, handle it calmly and with good humour, and carry on. In most cases, whatever happens will be obvious to your audience too, and they'll think all the more highly of you if they see that you're dealing gamely with difficult circumstances.

Your audience

Hecklers and protesters

If you're making a controversial speech, or representing a controversial organisation, you might have to deal with protesters. If someone has come a long way just to heckle you, it is unlikely that you can say anything to make them stop. But how you react can have a major effect on how the rest of your audience sees you.

The best thing to do is to assure the people who are protesting that they will have a chance to put any points or questions to you at the end of the speech, and ask them courteously to wait till then. It's important that you don't appear to be afraid of dissent, but at the same time you need to think of the majority of your audience, who have the right to hear you undisturbed.

If the protesters continue to disrupt your speech, don't try to fight them. Stop, don't look annoyed, and wait for the event organisers to deal with the situation. Make it clear that you've kept your good humour – a joke about the interruption afterwards will help to diffuse the tension. Recap if you need to – and carry on.

Responding to questions

Of all the different kinds of audience participation in your speech, one that you should always try to encourage is the asking of questions. Being open to questions from the floor sends an important message about your confidence in what you are saying, and inviting them also helps your speech to be more memorable. Audiences tend to pay more attention if they know that a speech will be discussed afterwards.

In an ideal world, of course, all the questions would be pertinent and appreciative, allowing you to expand on the points that your audience has been particularly intrigued by. In practice, things are rarely as simple as that. You may face long, rambling questions that don't really make sense, from people who don't sound as if they've been listening. There may be people who are more interested in standing up and making their own mini-speech, rather than asking you anything about yours. There may even be people who want to attack some of the things you said. Each of these audience responses needs to be handled in its own particular way.

With irrelevant or rambling questions, the important thing is to stay patient. However stupid the question might be, you need to treat the person who asked it with respect. If you're finding the question difficult to follow, try summarising it to see if you've got it right, and for the benefit of the rest of the audience.

If you think that someone's trying to hijack your speech by making their own points, it is important to try as soon as possible to shift the terms of the discussion back to where you want them to be. Phrases like 'I still think it's true that . . .' or 'I think my point still stands that . . .' are useful for doing this.

If someone asks you a question with what seems like aggressive intent, the important thing is to keep your cool. Don't meet hostility with hostility. Be calm and polite, and the audience will generally be on your side. Whatever the provocation, you need to appear to be more reasonable than the person who asked the question, more polite, more in control.

If you're asked a question to which you don't know the answer, be honest rather than trying to bluff. Promise to get back to the person who asked the question if it is something you can find out.

With all types of question, it's a good idea to repeat it (or para- phrase it) before you answer, for the benefit of people who didn't hear it the first time. And remember that generally it isn't the speaker's job to moderate questions – to hurry a long-winded questioner to make them get to the point, for example. Usually that's up to the event organisers.

Finally, it's always a good idea to work out in advance an intelligent question that the compère can ask you, in case there's nothing forth- coming from the floor.

Speaking through the media

It is a sad fact that the media, if they are going to report what you say, will probably give you only a 10-second clip on the TV or radio or a 50-word quote in a newspaper. These are the realities of the modern world, and if you think that your speech will attract media interest, you need to work within these limitations.

That means understanding the needs of the modern journalist. They want something short and snappy, which makes a point clearly in a few words. If you give them that, they may well use it.

So if you know that the media will be reporting your speech, look through your draft before you deliver it, and ask yourself which bits of it *you* would lift if you were a reporter working to a deadline. Make sure that somewhere in your speech there is a sparky phrase or two that neatly (and accurately) sums up what you're saying. Make sure that the bit of your speech that is easiest to quote or to broadcast is one which gets across your key message.

Normally this snappy summing-up should come near the end of your speech, so that as well as keeping the media happy it also helps your speech as a whole to build to a rousing finish. If you know, however, that there are reporters present who are on very tight deadlines, you might also want to drop something in earlier (ideally at the 'tell them what you're going to tell them' stage), so that they don't have to stay for the whole thing. With luck their resulting feelings of gratitude will colour the way they report your speech.

8 Speeches for all occasions

While the majority of the tips in this book apply to most types of speech, sometimes you have to speak in special circumstances, where there are particular things you need to bear in mind.

Speeches of welcome

Conferences and debates, sports days and training days – they all need someone to welcome people to them. If that someone is you, your first job is to make sure that your guests feel comfortable. Start with a few good jokes to break the ice. Recognise any particular efforts that certain people have made to be there. As well as your general welcome, include a special welcome if there are any special guests or speakers.

The next thing you need to do is to generate a sense of excitement about the day's events. Say something about the host organisation and what they do – people won't necessarily know. Provide an overview of the occasion, highlighting any particular items on the programme that you want to draw attention to (either because they're especially interesting, or because the organisers worry that they'll be poorly attended without a bit of extra advertising).

Conclude by saying that you hope everyone will enjoy themselves. Now's a good time to slip in the suggestion that guests follow up their participation in the event by joining the organisation that's hosting it, or signing up for a similar event, or agreeing to receive further information about forthcoming events . . .

Acceptance speeches

If you've been lucky enough to have won an award, be gracious and humble about it, but not so humble that you trivialise the award itself. Acknowledge the competition you were up against, and say how highly you rate the people you beat. Thank the people who are doing you the honour of giving you the award, and the people who helped you become so great at what you do. But don't gush, don't bawl, and try not to mention the Almighty too much in your list of thanks.

Farewell speeches

If you're the person who's leaving (changing job, for example), you need to say what it's meant to you, working with the people you've been working with, and share some of the newly developed skills, experiences and happy memories you're taking away with you. Say (diplomatically) why you have to go, and list some of the things you'll miss about the place you're leaving. Thank those who have helped you during your time at wherever-it-is, and give everyone your best wishes.

If you're talking on behalf of an organisation about someone who's leaving, express your gratitude for their contribution, and provide warm descriptions (if you can) of what they brought with them. Try to think of a few funny anecdotes that sum up the character of the person who's going. Talk about the gap that they'll leave behind them, and how difficult they'll be to replace (they probably won't know that their replacement is arriving next week).

Eulogies

Speeches given at a funeral or memorial service, in honour of the deceased, are of course among the most difficult to deliver. It doesn't matter if you cry. Just give yourself time, and be prepared to stop and wait until you're able to carry on.

Start by saying how you knew the person that you're talking about. Then describe them, remembering that you don't need to summarise everything they did in their life, just what really mattered to them and to the people you're addressing. And when it comes to the person's character, a few small details or anecdotes can be far more effective than general descriptions, in reminding people what their loved one was really like.

A eulogy doesn't have to paint the deceased as whiter-than-white, nor does it have to be entirely serious. Recalling a few of the funny things that someone said or did can be a very fitting tribute to them.

Wedding speeches

Why wedding speeches are easy

For many people, giving a speech at a wedding is their very first experience of public speaking in a formal setting. It's understandable if you're scared to death at the prospect. But before you start thinking about calling the whole thing off, there are a few things to remember.

First, compared to just about any other kind of public speaking, giving a speech at a wedding is a piece of cake. You know the audience, or at least some of them. They're there to have a good time, and they're in a good mood (and usually well lubricated by the time you stand up). Above all, they're on your side. They want you to succeed. They'll listen to you closely, and laugh if you give them half a chance. You don't have to change their minds about anything. All they want is to hear you say nice things about the bride and groom, and the bride and groom are people they know and care about already, otherwise they wouldn't be at the wedding.

The other great thing about speaking at weddings is that you're generally an expert on the subject you're talking about. That's why you're speaking, and not anyone else. You're talking about a side of the bride or groom that you know about, probably as well as anyone in the room. You have years of material to draw on. And best of all, you only have to talk for a few minutes.

That doesn't mean that wedding speeches are entirely effortless, of course, but all the elements that go towards speaking successfully at a wedding are under your control. Put the preparation in, judge the tone right and be yourself, and people will receive your words warmly and appreciatively.

Another thing to remember when you're asked to give a wedding speech is just how lucky you are. It doesn't matter if you're speaking in one of the more traditional roles – father of the bride, bride-groom, best man – or one of the less traditional ones (bride's best friend, for example) that feature increasingly in modern weddings. You don't get many opportunities in life to stand up in front of your friends and family and say what you really feel about someone you love.

So don't think about how nervous you are, or about what could go awry: think about the positive things. Get it wrong, and people will probably be too drunk to remember anyway. Get it right, and they'll remember what you say for the rest of their lives.

The descriptions of the main wedding speech roles that follow are based on the traditional pattern of weddings in the UK. If it's your wedding and you have some choice in the matter, don't feel that you have to follow this pattern strictly. It's easy to get intimidated by the formalities surrounding wedding speeches, but wedding guests these days are used to hearing speeches from a wide variety of people. If there's someone who you really want to speak, by all means ask them to. Traditions can be moulded to suit you.

It's useful to bear in mind, though, that the traditional pattern of bride's father followed by groom followed by best man is what people are used to, and it's what they'll be expecting. It also creates a dynamic between the speeches, moving from the more touching reminiscences of the bride's father and the tributes of the groom, to the more knock-about humour of the best man. If you're going to have additional speeches, or if you otherwise alter the roles of the people who speak, it's a good idea still to follow this basic pattern. If the bride wants her chief bridesmaid to speak, for example, this speech will probably be closest in style to the best man's, so it makes sense to put it near the end of the speeches. A favourite uncle would most naturally speak shortly after the bride's father, since his speech will probably be quite similar. The bride may want to speak as well as the groom rather than having other people speak for her; if so, logically, she should speak shortly before or after him. In the case of civil partnerships, both partners will probably want to speak in the 'groom' slot.

The basic functions of the different speeches heard at a traditional wedding may appear arbitrary, but they've developed over hundreds of years, and there are very good reasons for them being as they are. If you're going to depart from tradition, it's important to understand what these underlying reasons are, so that the speeches you come up with still fit in with them.

The traditional wedding speech roles make sense from the point of view of the guests, and they're largely about smoothing over areas of potential conflict. A successful wedding speech is therefore one that reassures the guests on a number of important points.

They want to know, first of all, that they're really welcome at the event they've been invited to. They want to hear that from the person who is paying for it all (traditionally the bride's father) and they want it to sound sincere. Then they want to know that the bride's father is happy about the reason for all of this – that he and his family fully accept the newcomer, the groom. Finally, they want to hear how much the bride has been loved and supported by her family. They want to believe that families work, and that marriages work.

Much of the groom's speech (and the best man's too, for that matter) is all about reassuring those people who don't know him about the person who has come to take the blushing bride away. The guests want to know that this is someone who recognises and is grateful for everything that has been done during the process of organising the wedding. They want to hear that his family are supportive, and that he appreciates that fact. They want to hear that the groom gets on with the bride's family and is happy to be considered a part of that family. Finally, the wedding guests want to be reassured that the groom is devoted to his bride.

The best man's job, once all of this tricky ground has been negotiated, and everyone is feeling confident that this is going to be a happy marriage that will last, is to get people laughing and enjoying themselves. The best man's role is also to help make the groom look more human and less threatening to those who don't know him. That's why the humour is generally at his expense, and comes from someone who has known him for a long time, and yet who clearly has great affection for him.

It can be tremendously jarring if any of these elements is missing. Hearing a bride's father crack some great jokes, welcome everyone warmly, pay moving tribute to his daughter, and yet conspicuously say nothing about liking or approving of his new son-in-law, can be a very uncomfortable experience.

That's why it's important not to shirk your responsibility to cover the ground that you need to cover. It may be very tempting to do the bare minimum – to mumble a few thank yous, and say that all of you who are giving speeches have agreed to keep them short. But it creates a very bad impression if you appear to be ducking out of saying what you need to say.

Being yourself

With wedding speeches more than any other, it's important to be yourself. That means not using stock lines from books or websites, not using corny one-liners that have clearly been pinched. You're speaking at a wedding because you know the bride or groom uniquely well, and the very least you can do is to put yourself into your speech, rather than using someone else's words.

Avoiding offence

Once you know that your speech covers everything it needs to, you must think carefully about whether there is anything in it that could possibly upset anyone. The one great pitfall that wedding speeches need to avoid is labelled 'offence'. You can give offence in many different ways, and wedding guests being what they are, you can guarantee that if you give offence there will be somebody at the wedding who will take it.

Avoiding offence means starting with the basics. On a formal level, check with the bride and groom what your role will be within the proceedings – who you're supposed to thank, to toast, to hand over to. Ask the bride and groom whether there are any family sensitivities that you should be aware of. Double-check that you've got people's names right, including how they're pronounced. And keep off the alcohol, at least until your speech is over – no blurting anything out that you shouldn't under the influence of the demon drink.

Gathering material for a wedding speech

More than with most types of speech, wedding speeches work best when they're based on the personal reminiscences of the person who's talking. That means that you are carrying around most of what you need for your speech already, in your own head. You can help the process along by talking to other people who know the bride or groom well. But chiefly what you need to do is to write down all of the most entertaining and touching observations and anecdotes that you've accumulated over however many years it is that you've known them.

Start yourself off thinking about the person you'll be speaking about, and be ready (with a notepad by your bed, another next to your bath . . .) to capture all the stray memories that your unconscious throws up, between now and the big day. Be prepared for the fact that this is likely to happen at the oddest times and in the most inconvenient places.

Among all the material you could use, what are you looking for? First, something that tells your listeners about the stars of the show, the bride and groom. Your speech shouldn't really be about you, except incidentally. Upstaging the happy couple won't win you many friends. It helps if you don't repeat what one of the other speakers has already said, so try to get together with them before the wedding, to check that there's no duplication between your speeches.

Next, you want to find things that are funny. Wedding speeches need anecdotes, not one-liners. And remember – though many of the guests may be strangers to you, most of them know the bride or groom well enough to have been invited, so it won't take much for them to find a quirky story about the newly-weds very funny indeed. Using props is a good way of injecting humour into a wedding speech – some of the groom's toys from when he was a child, for example, to illustrate particular character traits.

But ultimately, your speech needs to be sweet. If you're mocking some of the groom's characteristics, you should do so with affection. If you're recounting an embarrassing story, it mustn't be so embarrassing as to cause offence to any of your listeners, and it needs to say something about the person concerned that is ultimately endearing.

Lastly, don't talk for too long. Standing between wedding guests and a free bar is a dangerous place to be.

Traditional roles for wedding speeches

The father of the bride

The bride's father (or whoever gives the bride away) makes what is largely a speech of welcome. Traditionally, the father of the bride is the person who pays for everything, so it is his job to welcome all the guests and thank them for coming. The listeners will also want and expect to hear the bride's father welcome the groom into his family – he should

SPEECHES FOR ALL OCCASIONS

try to sound reasonably enthusiastic about this, even if he isn't. Finally, the bride's father's job is to pay tribute to his daughter, to talk about what she was like growing up, and in many cases to pull the groom's leg about what he's letting himself in for. The speech concludes with a toast to the bride and groom.

Starting points: the father of the bride's speech

- Has anything funny happened in organising the reception – a mix-up with the caterers, say, or the wrong live band being booked?

- Has anyone gone beyond the call of duty, and come to the wedding from especially far away, or surmounted significant obstacles to be there?

- What are your happiest memories of your daughter when she was growing up?

- What strong personality traits does your daughter have, and what advice can you give the groom in dealing with these?

- When did you first hear about and then meet the groom, and what were your first impressions of him?

- Finally, what would you like to say to your daughter, and what would you like to wish her?

The groom

The groom's job primarily is to thank people. Traditionally, since he's following on from the bride's father, the groom starts by thanking him for what he's just said about welcoming him into the family. He often pays tribute to his own family, and the support they've given him, and he thanks everyone who's been involved in paying for, organising and officiating at the wedding (often the two sets of parents, plus bridesmaids, ushers etc). Finally, the groom lavishes praise on his bride, and says how happy he is to be marrying her. The groom's speech traditionally ends with a toast to the brides-maids.

Starting points: the groom's speech

- Is there anything in the bride's father's speech that you could pick up on, or make a joke out of?

- What do you need to thank your bride's family for? For organising and paying for the event? For welcoming you as a son-in-law?

- Have your new parents-in-law given you any advice about your bride, or about married life?

- What do you need to thank your own family for?

- Who else needs to be thanked – bridesmaids, ushers, your best man ... ?

- Finally, what made you fall in love with your bride? What would you like to say to her?

The best man

Of course, the father of the bride and the groom will often try to weave some jokes into their speeches, but it's primarily the best man's job to be entertaining. In a formal sense he may have jobs to do, such as replying on behalf of the bridesmaids to the nice things that the groom has just said about them, reading out messages from people who couldn't be there, and acting as the Master of Ceremonies for the rest of the day's entertainment. But the best man's main job is to talk about the groom, and to be funny while he's doing it. The best man's speech finishes with a toast to the bride and groom.

Starting points: the best man's speech

- What is the groom like as a person?

- What was he like when he was younger?

- How did he try to impress his bride when they first met?

- When and how did you first know that he was serious about her?

- How has he changed (for the better) since meeting her?

- What does it mean to you to have been asked to be best man?

- What would you like to wish the happy couple?

Sample wedding speech

Finally, here's a great example of a real wedding speech. It was given by my friend Lucy, when she married my friend Robin.

What's so good about it? First, it's a rare example of a speech which promises to be brief, and sticks to that promise.

More importantly, it doesn't have a single line in it that sounds as if it's been borrowed from someone else. Everything in the speech rings true for the speaker, and even the ice-breaker says something specific-ally about her, making it especially funny for anyone who knows her.

More importantly still, the speech manages to take some of the stock romantic phrases – 'I love you', 'you're beautiful' – and make them sound absolutely sincere. That's quite an impressive feat for a short wedding speech.

The speech incorporates a nice sight gag (Lucy takes out a piece of paper to read a poem, but it turns out that the poem only has one line). The joke makes a bigger point, though, about trying to find your own words to express your feelings, rather than relying on someone else's.

This, in fact, was the first stage in the process of writing the speech: Lucy had been looking for a poem that said what she wanted to say, but she hadn't been able to find one that fitted the bill, and even when she tried to write her own it didn't sound natural. So she decided to abandon the attempt, but in abandoning it she found the theme that the speech hinges on.

Lucy fixes on a small aspect of her life with Robin – the fact that he makes her a cup of tea every morning. It's funny when it's read out as a line in a poem, because it seems so banal. But as the speech goes on, this little daily act of kindness comes to seem anything but trivial. Again, it's a real, concrete detail – the absolute opposite of cliché – which makes the speech sound sincere. And as Lucy says, she wanted her speech to reflect the idea that marriage is about routine, as well as about the spectacle of the wedding day.

The theme of the cup of tea also chimes perfectly with the point in the day's events when the speech was given. Lucy was speaking as the wedding guests were standing with cups of tea in their hands, before the wedding ceremony and the more traditional speeches of the groom and best man, which came later. The toast of tea, then, is an original but very fitting way of rounding the speech off.

Giving a speech as a bride is still relatively unusual, and Lucy spends some time acknowledging this, and explaining (with plenty of self-deprecating humour) why she's doing it. Because the bride isn't expected to speak, though, Lucy was able to focus on what she actually wanted to say, rather than being distracted by the thought that she 'had to give a speech'.

This is a beautiful example of how you can give a speech in front of a large group of people and make it funny and moving for them, while at the same time speaking very directly to an individual. Here's the speech in full:

Don't worry, don't worry. I'll keep this brief. Despite my recent appearance in the commercial for New Woman magazine, I'm not ready for my Oscar speech yet.

I know it isn't traditional for a bride to make a speech, but I thought I'd say a few words for two reasons.

First because, in this post-feminist, equal opportunities world, it seems a shame for a gobby woman like me to keep quiet while the men in her life talk on her behalf.

And secondly because I think that the traditional speeches mean that the groom doesn't get a look in. Sure, he gets to make a speech, thanking the bridesmaids, and telling the bride how beautiful and lovely she looks (I hope you're taking notes, Robin). And he'll get ribbed a bit by his best man. But he doesn't have anyone who stands up and says how marvellous he is.

Call me crazy, but given that I'm marrying you today sweetie, I thought I'd give it a go. And in honour of you, and of our love, I thought I'd write you a poem. I thought long and hard about our relationship, and here it is.

[Opens up a piece of paper]

It's called 'Every Morning You Make Me a Cup of Tea'. And it starts:

'Every morning you make me a cup of tea.'

But it doesn't go any further, because every time I tried to follow that up with my thoughts about us, everything sounded too much like a cliché. So I scrapped the poem idea and thought I'd just tell the truth.

Robin, you are all the things that boys hate to be called: you are cute, you're beautiful, you're kind, you're sweet, you're sensitive, and you're really, really nice.

You are also everything that a man should be: you are considerate, strong, brave, honest, and loyal. Loyal to me, and loyal to <u>us</u>.

You are my best friend, and the last five years have been the happiest of my life. I love being in a gang with you and being part of a family, and I'm proud to make our little gang official today by becoming your wife.

Given the kind impression that you've made on me by always waking me up in the morning with a smile and a cuppa, I think it is only appropriate that we start our wedding day with a cup of tea. And one you haven't made, and don't even have to wash up later. And I hope that as you and all our lovely guests take a sip, they'll make a silent toast to you my love:

To Robin, the most beautiful man in the room.

Perfect Letters and Emails for All Occasions

George Davidson

All you need to get it right first time

- Do you sometimes find it difficult to get your message across in emails?
- Are you worried that your formal letters are letting you down?
- Do you want some straightforward advice on improving your writing skills?

Perfect Letters and Emails for All Occasions is an invaluable guide for anyone who wants to get the most out of their written communication. Covering everything from advice on how to write to your MP to tips about 'netiquette' and avoiding offensive blunders, it is a one-stop-shop for anyone who wants their writing to get results. Whether you're sending a reply to a formal invitation or a covering letter for a job application, *Perfect Letters and Emails for All Occasions* has all you need to make sure you get your message across elegantly and effectively.

BOOKS

Perfect Wedding Speeches and Toasts

George Davidson

All you need to give a brilliant speech

- Have you been asked to 'say a few words' on the big day and don't quite know how to go about it?
- Do you want easy-to-follow tips on making a speech that is both meaningful and memorable?
- Do you want some guidance on how to improve your skills as a public speaker?

Perfect Wedding Speeches and Toasts is an invaluable guide to preparing and delivering unforgettable speeches. Covering everything from advice on mastering your nerves to tips about how to make a real impact, it walks you through every aspect of preparing for the big day and speaking in public. Whether you're the father of the bride, the bride herself, or the best man, *Perfect Wedding Speeches and Toasts* will help make sure your speech goes off without a hitch.

rh

BOOKS

Order titles in the *Perfect* series
from your local bookshop, or have them delivered
direct to your door by Bookpost.

☐ Perfect Best Man	George Davidson	9781905211784	£5.99
☐ Perfect Interview	Max Eggert	9781905211746	£7.99
☐ Perfect Letters and Emails for All Occasions	George Davidson	9781847945495	£6.99
☐ Perfect Persuasion	Richard Storey	9781847945594	£7.99
☐ Perfect Presentations	Andrew Leigh and Michael Maynard	9781844130207	£6.99
☐ Perfect Punctuation	Stephen Curtis	9781905211685	£6.99
☐ Perfect Readings for Weddings	Jonathan Law	9781905211098	£6.99
☐ Perfect Wedding Speeches and Toasts	George Davidson	9781905211777	£5.99
☐ Perfect Written English	Chris West	9781847945037	£6.99

Free post and packing
Overseas customers allow £2 per paperback

Phone: 01624 677237

Post: Random House Books
c/o Bookpost, PO Box 29, Douglas, Isle of Man IM99 1BQ

Fax: 01624 670 923

email: bookshop@enterprise.net

Cheques (payable to Bookpost) and credit cards accepted

Prices and availability subject to change without notice.
Allow 28 days for delivery.
When placing your order, please state if you do not
wish to receive any additional information.

www.rbooks.co.uk

BOOKS